GRAMMAR EXERCISES

Part Two
Intermediate ESL

David P. Rein

illustrations by Robert MacLean

Interplay ESL

PRO LINGUA ASSOCIATES

Publishers

Published by Pro Lingua Associates
15 Elm Street
Brattleboro, Vermont 05301
802-257-7779

SAN 216-0579

Also in the *Interplay ESL* series:

Grammar Handbook: Part One by Nancy Clair
Grammar Exercises: Part One by Arthur A. Burrows
Grammar Handbook: Part Two by Nancy Clair
Grammar Handbook: Part Three —forthcoming
Grammar Exercises: Part Three —forthcoming
Smalltown Daily: an elementary/intermediate/advanced
 reader edited by John N. Miller and Raymond C. Clark

Copyright © 1986 by David P. Rein

All rights reserved. No part of this publication may be represented or transmitted in any form or by any means, electronic, mechanical, photocopying, recording, or other, or stored in an information storage or retrieval system except for classroom use, without permission in writing from the publisher.

ISBN 0-86647-014-X

This book was set by David Chase of Brattleboro, Vermont, with display type in Century Oldstyle and the cover and title page in Tiffany set by Stevens Graphics of Brattleboro. It was printed and bound by The Murray Printing Company in Kendallsville, Indiana. Designed by Arthur A. Burrows.

Printed in the United States of America.

Contents

Preface on *Interplay ESL*   vii
Introduction   ix
General   1

   1. Negative (YES/NO) questions   1
      Music and musicians

   2. Reported speech I: commands and statements   6
      Dates and appointments

   3. Reported speech II: questions   9
      Currency

   4. HOW and WHAT questions   13
      Growing things

   5. Compound sentences: short additions   16
      with BUT; TOO, SO, EITHER, NEITHER
      Getting acquainted

   6. Review of tag questions   20
      Around the world in 67 days

Nouns   24

   7. Agent suffixes   24
      Occupations

   8. Abstract nouns   27
      Quotations

Pronouns   30

   9. -SELF/-SELVES pronouns   30
      Social relations

   10. Impersonal pronouns   32
      Driving

   11. Indefinite compound pronouns   35
      Fear, jealousy, and suspicion

   12. Quantity words with partitives I: 38
      ONE, ANOTHER, THE OTHER
      A picnic

   13. Quantity words with partitives II: 41
      Pleasure and satisfaction

   14. Anticipatory IT   46
      New York City

Verbs   50

15. Future time without future tense   50
    Extracurricular activities
16. Past progressive tense   53
    A waiter's life
17. Present perfect tense   56
    Tooth troubles
18. Past perfect tense   61
    Ancient history
19. Future perfect and perfect   64
    progressive forms
    Class reunion
20. Customary past (USED TO, WOULD)   68
    and present (BE USED TO)
    Changing times
21. Past of GOING TO and ABOUT TO   72
    Accidents and injuries
22. Modals of obligation and necessity: 75
    HAVE TO, MUST
    At a hospital
23. Modals of advisability and obligation: 79
    SHOULD, OUGHT TO, HAD BETTER
    Household chores
24. Modals of preference: WOULD RATHER,   83
    WOULD LIKE
    Washington, D.C.
25. Modals of possibility: CAN, COULD,   86
    MAY, MIGHT
    Picking out a gift
26. Modals of probability and inference   89
    SHOULD/OUGHT TO, MUST
    Drawing conclusions
27. Modal of obligation and expectation: 92
    BE SUPPOSED TO
    The medicine cabinet
28. Modals in the past   95
    Mistakes and regrets
29. Review of modals   99
    Study habits and homework

30. Nonseparable two-word verbs   104
Headlines

31. Causative: MAKE, HAVE, GET   107
Goods and services

32. Passive voice I: present and future time   111
Sciences

33. Passive voice II: past and perfect tenses   115
Disease

34. Gerunds   119
Exercise

35. Verb + gerund   123
A life of crime

36. Verb + infinitive   127
Teachers

37. Verb + gerund or infinitive   131
Hobbies

38. Verb + simple or progressive forms   135
Private eye (P.I.)

39. DO vs. MAKE   139
Entertaining guests

40. Participles as adjectives (-ING vs. -ED)   143
Plays

Adjectives and adverbs   145

41. Comparative constructions   145
A family

42. Adverbs of time: STILL, ANYMORE, ALREADY, YET   148
Old age

43. Adverbs of degree: VERY, TOO, ENOUGH   152
Weights and measures

44. Word order of adverbials   155
Museums

Prepositions   160

45. Miscellaneous prepositions   160
Tips for householders

46. Prepositions in fixed phrases   164
Mr. Crabbe's opinions

Clauses   **167**

    47. Adjective clauses   167
         The dating game

    48. Adverb clauses of time   170
         Autobiography

    49. Adverb clauses of reason   173
        and concession
         Natural wonders

    50. Conditional clauses: real   176
         Etiquette

    51. Conditional clauses: unreal   180
         Card and board games

    52. Noun clauses with HOPE and WISH   185
         Possibilities

Appendices: **189**

    Irregular verb forms   189
    Some nonseparable two-word verbs   190
    A summary of verb tenses   191
    Some useful spelling rules   192

Answers to the exercises   **193**

Grammar and key word index   **209**

Cultural topic index   **212**

Preface on Interplay ESL

Grammar Exercises: Part Two is the fourth in a collection of language textbooks we will be publishing over the next few years as the *Interplay for ESL* series. This ESL collection, once it is complete, will be a unique set of language materials that answers the needs of teachers who are looking for books that liberate, rather than restrict, the teacher, and encourage creativity in the classroom. The ESL collection will eventually form a comprehensive curriculum that will meet the needs of students ranging from the absolute beginner level to the advanced level.

Although the *Interplay for ESL* series as a total package will be based on a coordinated plan, it will also be distinguished by the fact that it is a modular program. Each and every book in the series can stand alone and is not rigidly linked to nor dependent on other books in the series. This book, for example, can be used by itself as an interesting and creative way to explore the grammar of English. It can also be used in close coordination with Pro Lingua Associates' *The Grammar Handbook: Part Two* or to supplement or complement other ESL textbooks.

Interplay for ESL as a complete curriculum will be divided into two stages. Stage One, The Introductory Course, will be a short, integrated program designed for the beginning student with little or no English. Stage Two, the Basic Course, begins at the elementary level and will proceed to the advanced level. There will be two basic modules at each level of the Basic Course. One will be the grammar module; the other will be based on a communicative syllabus. In addition, there will be supplementary modules for strengthening the following skill areas: Conversation, Pronunciation, Listening Comprehension, Writing, Vocabulary, and Reading. A text for the last of these modules, Reading, is already available. *The Smalltown Daily* is a multilevel reader based on newspaper articles of general interest.

There are two books at the intermediate level of the grammar module of the Basic Course. *Grammar Exercises: Part Two* and *The Grammar Handbook: Part Two* are designed to be used together or independently. The former is a self-study or homework text; the latter, for classroom use. They cover the same grammar point for point. The Part Two module is also designed to follow the books in Part One although, again, this is not necessary. Part One is aimed specifically at "The false beginner" or elementary-intermediate students, and it presents grammar for elementary and low intermediate study. These Part Two books cover grammar points taught in intermediate to high intermediate courses.

For more information on how to use this unique text/workbook, we urge you to study the author's introduction and the first, explanatory lesson carefully.

Pro Lingua Associates
Arthur A. Burrows
Raymond C. Clark
Patrick R. Moran

Introduction

The method of *Grammar Exercises: Part Two* can be summarized by these seven points:

1. **This book is designed for independent study or homework.**
   It can be used in the classroom, but the teacher will want to rely on its companion text, *The Grammar Handbook: Part Two,* or other resources for a full classroom presentation and in-class practice.

2. **Each lesson has both a grammatical and a topical focus.**
   For example, Lesson 23 presents the modals of advisability, but it also works with information and vocabulary related to typical household chores. Why? It is our contention that by building grammar exercises using sentences which are all interrelated and focused on some entertaining and culturally stimulating topic, we can engage the imagination of students and put them into an acquisitive frame of mind.

3. **The book is appropriate for intermediate study.**
   It is for the intermediate to high intermediate student. It can be used for initial presentation or review.

4. The exercises vary in difficulty.
The first exercises in each lesson provide the intermediate student with practice on the basic grammar point of the lesson. Students can then go on to be challenged by the more difficult exercises at the end of the lesson.

5. There are more than enough exercises.
The students do not have to complete each lesson. Although some students may become involved with the cultural topic and want to work their way through all the exercises and vocabulary, they should not be required to do so.

6. Answers to most of the exercises are given in the appendix.
The students should be encouraged to check their answers, to puzzle out their errors using the grammar explanations, and then to make all the corrections. The teacher can then encourage them to bring any problems they cannot work out on their own for explanation and discussion in class. By correcting their own work, the students get feedback immediately, when it is most effective. The students are thus encouraged to become self-reliant in their study and to treat their teacher, classmates, and English-speaking friends as resources.

7. The sequencing of lessons is flexible.
The student or class can take up the grammar points as they are needed, coordinating this book with most curriculum designs. The lessons follow the order of the classroom presentations in *The Grammar Handbook: Part Two* point for point, although the grammar is explained here in somewhat greater detail than would be appropriate in classroom paradigms. Used in conjunction with the classroom handbook, these lessons thus offer both a reinforcement and an enrichment of the class activities.

In keeping with the underlying concepts of **Interplay,*** this book is intended to be learner-centered, to be flexible and fun, and to stimulate a free exchange of ideas between the students, their teacher, and their friends in and out of class.

*See "Interplay" in the appendix of *Language Teaching Techniques*, Raymond C. Clark; Pro Lingua Associates, Publishers; 1980; pp. 117-120.

GRAMMAR EXERCISES

Part Two

1 Negative (YES/NO) questions

Music and musicians

We form negative questions by contracting **not** and the form of **be** or the auxiliary verb.

***Wasn't** the trumpet solo the best part of the program?*
***Haven't** you ever heard the Boston Symphony Orchestra?*
***Won't** anyone give $5,000 to the musicians' fund?*

We use negative questions with contractions chiefly to:

1. confirm an idea or an opinion.

    A: ***Wasn't** that their worst concert of the season?*
    B: *Yes, it certainly was.*
    A: ***I thought so too.***

2. express surprise.

    A: ***Aren't** you a Beatles fan?*
    B: *No, I'm not.*
    A: *I'm surprised. I thought you were.*

3. correct or remind someone gently; make a gentle suggestion to someone.

    A: *Beethoven wrote ten symphonies.*
    B: ***Didn't** he write only nine?*

    A: ***Shouldn't** that be an A flat, not an A natural?*
    B: *You're right, it should.*

1 Negative (YES/NO) questions

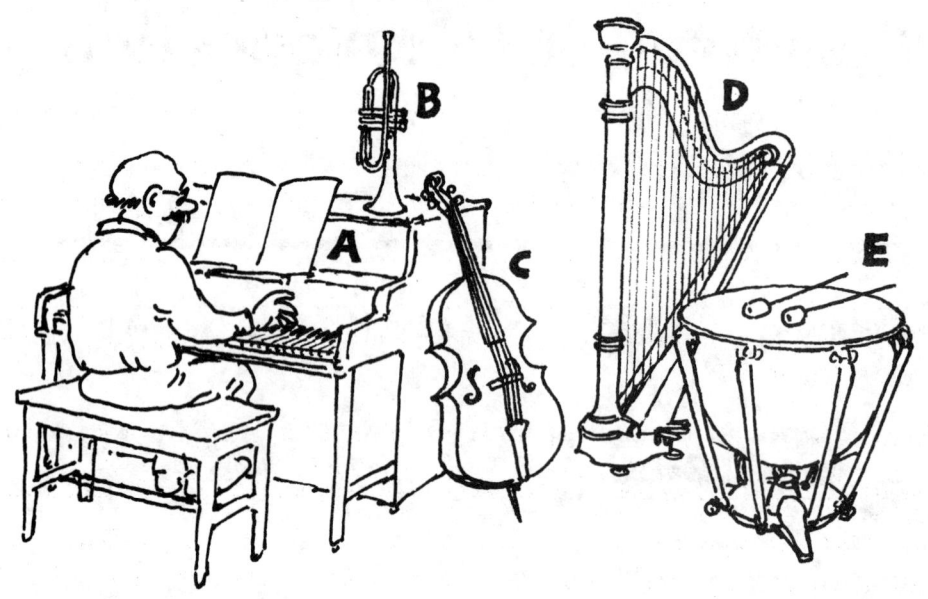

Can you name these instruments? A _____ B. _____
C. _____ D. _____ E. _____

A. Rewrite each statement of an idea or an opinion as a negative question.

I think that was an exciting concert.
Wasn't that an exciting concert?

1. I think the Bach family was the most important one in musical history.
   _____

2. I think Handel's oratorios are the most inspired ones ever written.
   _____

3. I think the French horn is the most beautiful instrument in the orchestra.
   _____

4. I think Shostakovich's music was banned by Stalin.
   _____

5. I think the string section sounds better than usual tonight.
   _____

6. I think the orchestra should play more twentieth-century music.
   _____

Negative (YES/NO) questions 1

7. I think Culture Club is going to be in town next Friday.

8. I think they have an excellent concert series here, for such a small city.

B. Change the first sentence in each pair to a negative question. Don't change the second sentence.

I'm surprised that you can't play the piano. I thought you could.

Can't you play the piano? I thought you could.

1. I'm surprised that you don't like Billy Joel. I thought you did.

2. I'm surprised that Jeff isn't a Michael Jackson fan. I thought he was.

3. I'm surprised that Brahms didn't write more than four symphonies. I thought he had.

4. I'm surprised you won't play a duet with me. I thought you would.

5. I'm surprised that Mozart wasn't older than thirty-five when he died. I thought he was.

6. I'm surprised that the English horn isn't a brass instrument. I thought it was.

7. I'm surprised that Barry Manilow doesn't like to be on TV. I thought he did.

8. I'm surprised that you aren't interested in music. I thought you were.

1 Negative (YES/NO) questions 4

C. Soften these corrections by **changing** them to negative questions. Use the clues in parentheses.

Brahms didn't write "Ode to Joy." (Beethoven)
Didn't Beethoven write "Ode to Joy"?

1. John Lennon wasn't the Beatles' drummer. (Ringo Starr)

2. You don't play a harp by **hitting** the strings. (plucking)

3. C.P.E. Bach wasn't **J.S. Bach's father.** (son)

4. Segovia didn't play the **cello.** (guitar)

5. The piccolo doesn't **have a lower range than the flute.** (higher)

Negative (YES/NO) questions

D. Soften these reminders and suggestions by changing them to negative questions.

It's time for the concert to begin.
Isn't it time for the concert to begin?

1. You can play your drums a little softer.

2. That should be played in the key of C.

3. It's a good idea to get concert tickets in advance.

4. You should practice the Chopin preludes.

5. You can play your violin tomorrow.

Vocabulary Summary

brass	flute	oratorio	series
cello	French horn	orchestra	solo
concert	harp	piano	string
drum	instrument	piccolo	symphony
drummer	key	play (v.)	trumpet
duet	music	prelude	tune (v.)
English horn	musical	program	violin
fan	musician	range	

2 Reported speech I

Dates and appointments

1. Like direct commands (imperative), reported commands may be either affirmative or negative. Use infinitive forms for reported commands.

   Affirmative — infinitive

   Mrs. Graves to Mr. Graves: "Please **call** Dr. Madison for an appointment." (direct)*
   *Mrs. Graves told Mr. Graves **to call** Dr. Madison for an appointment. (reported)*

   *Please makes a direct command more polite, but it is seldom used in reported commands.

   Negative — **not** + infinitive

   *Mrs. Graves to Mr. Graves: **"Don't put** it **off."** (direct)*
   *Mrs. Graves told Mr. Graves **not to put** it **off.** (reported)*

   When changing from direct commands to reported commands, adjust the persons.

   *Mrs. Graves to **Mr. Graves:** "Please call Dr. Madison for an appointment for **me**."*
   *Mrs. Graves told **her husband** to call Dr. Madison for an appointment for **her**.*

   Direct speech can include reported speech.

   Mr. Graves to Dr. Madison's receptionist: "My wife asked me to call for an appointment for her."

2. A speaker's direct statement may also be reported to another person.

   Mr. Graves to Mrs. Graves: "Your appointment is for four o'clock Wednesday." (direct)
   Mr. Graves is telling Mrs. Graves (that)* her appointment is for four o'clock Wednesday. (reported)

   *That is optional.

   When changing from direct statements to reported statements, adjust the persons and the tenses.

   *Mr. Graves **said**, **"Martha, your** appointment **is** for four o'clock Wednesday."*
   *Mr. Graves **is telling his wife** (that) **her** appointment **is** for four o'clock Wednesday.*
   *Mr. Graves **told his wife** (that) **her** appointment **was** for four o'clock Wednesday.*

7 Reported speech: commands and statements 2

A. Mrs. Graves owns a small store with three employees. She recently announced a meeting. Rewrite her instructions as reported commands, using **told**.

Meet me after closing Thursday.
She told them to meet her after closing Thursday.

1. Don't miss the meeting.

2. Be ready with the week's sales figures.

3. Plan to stay no more than an hour.

4. Don't forget about the meeting.

B. This is a conversation between Mrs. Graves and her hairdresser, Pierre. Rewrite it in one paragraph as reported speech, using **says**.

Pierre, I need to make an appointment to have my hair done. I want to look really special. I'm going to an important dinner Saturday.

I can see you in an hour, Mrs. Graves.

I'm sorry, but I can't be there then. We're having a big sale, and I can't leave the store.

I can give you an appointment Friday at 4:30.

That will be fine.

2 Reported speech: commands and statements   8

Mrs. Graves says she needs to make an appointment to have her hair done. She says
_____
_____
_____
_____
_____
_____
_____

C. Now write the conversation in Exercise B as reported speech using **said**.

Mrs. Graves said she needed to make an appointment to have her hair done.
_____
_____
_____
_____
_____
_____
_____

D. Write **said** or **told** in each blank.

   Mrs. Graves _____ her husband she wasn't feeling well at all. She ____ him to call the doctor for an appointment. He _____ that he would. When Mr. Graves called, Dr. Madison's receptionist _____ the doctor was completely booked for Tuesday. However, she _____ Mr. Graves that the doctor was free Wednesday at 4. Mr. Graves _____ that would be fine. After he hung up, he _____ his wife that she had an appointment for Wednesday at 4. She ____ that she was feeling much worse and she wasn't sure she could wait that long.

Vocabulary Summary

appointment	free	meeting	receptionist
booked	employee	put (something)	
date	instruction	off	

Reported speech II 3

Currency

Reported questions use statement word order: subject before verb.

> **statement:** ***There are*** *100 cents in a U.S. dollar.*
> **direct question:** *"How many cents **are there** in a U.S. dollar?"*
> **reported question:** *Torwald is asking how many cents **there are** in a U.S. dollar.*

Reported yes/no questions use **whether** or **if**.

> *Torwald: "Is a dime or a nickel worth five cents?"* (direct)
> *Torwald is asking **whether/if** a dime or a nickel is worth five cents.* (reported)

When changing from direct questions to reported questions, adjust the persons and the tenses.

> *Torwald to Olaf: **"Do you have** change for a quarter?"* (direct)
> *Torwald asked Olaf whether/if **he had** change for a quarter.* (reported)

Reported questions may be embedded in statements or in questions with verbs other than **ask**.

> *I wonder*
> *I'd like to know*   } *how much a nickel is worth.*
> *I can't remember*   } *whether/if it's worth five cents or ten.*
> *Nobody can tell me*

> *Don't you wonder*
> *Do you know*   } *how much a nickel is worth?*
> *Do you remember*   } *whether/if it's worth five cents or ten?*
> *Can anybody tell me*

A. Change André's direct questions to reported questions with **is asking**.

"What coin do I need for a pay phone?"
André is asking what coin he needs for a pay phone.

"Does anyone have change for a dollar?"
He is asking if anyone has change for a dollar.

1. "Aren't there four quarters in a U.S. dollar?"

   _____

3 Reported speech: questions

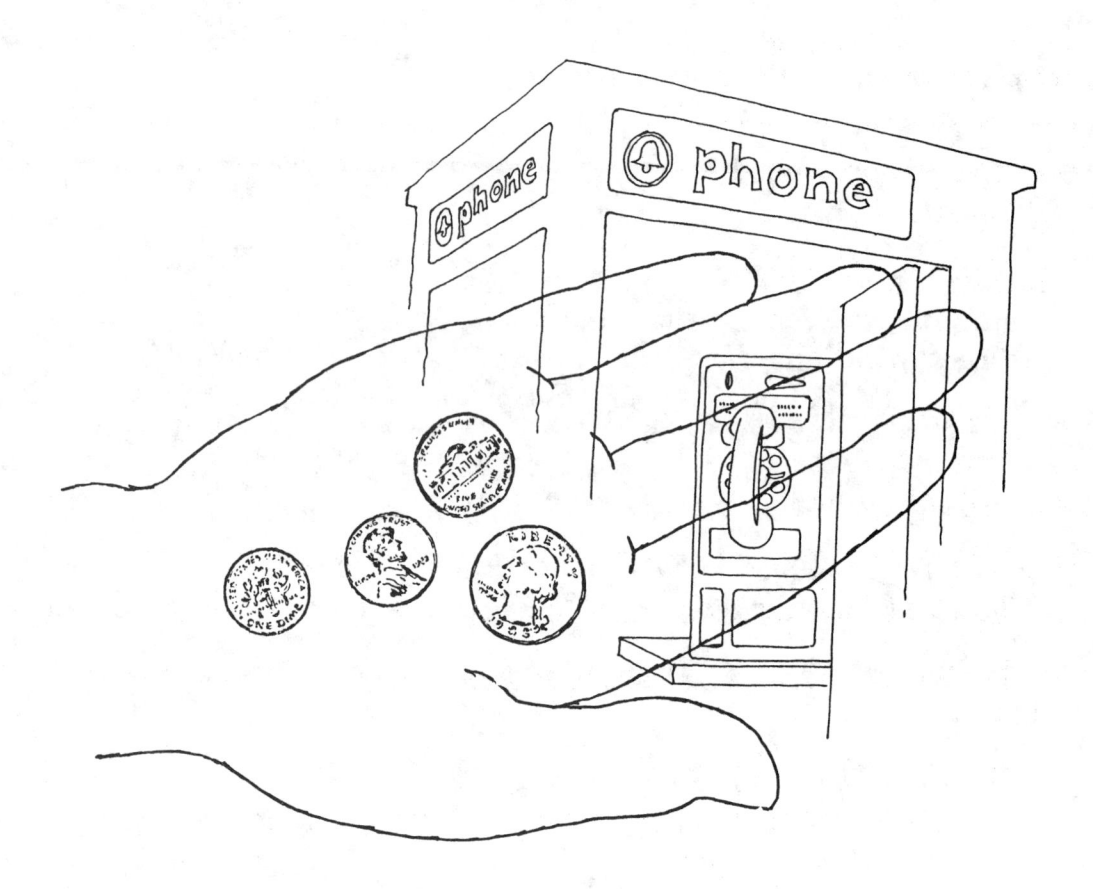

2. "Why did somebody give me only three?"

3. "How many dollars can I get for a hundred francs?"

4. "Can anybody change a hundred-franc bill for me?"

5. "Will the cashier do it?"

6. "Where can I exchange my French money?"

7. "What's the name of the bank?"

8. "How far away is that?"

9. "Does anyone want to go to the bank with me?"

10. "What kind of friends do I have?"

11 Reported speech: questions 3

B. This is a conversation between Laurie and her friend Don. Rewrite it in one paragraph as reported speech, using **asked** and **said**.

Laurie: When are you leaving for Europe, Don?

Don: I'm going Tuesday.

Laurie: Which countries are you visiting?

Don: Italy is the only one. I'm staying with relatives there.

Laurie: Do you have any Italian money yet?

Don: I'm going to the bank for some on Friday.

Laurie: What kind of money do they use there?

Don: They use lire.

Laurie: What's the exchange rate?

Don: There are 1920 lire to a dollar, according to the morning paper.

Laurie asked Don when he was leaving for Europe

TABLE 1

TABLE 1: CURRENCY CONVERSIONS

AUSTRIA
22.09 Schillings = U.S. $1
100 Groschen = 1 Schilling

BRAZIL
3041 cruzeiros = U.S. $1
100 centavos = 1 cruzeiro

COLOMBIA
96.15 pesos = U.S. $1
100 centavos = 1 peso

EGYPT
.7690 pounds = U.S. $1
100 piastres = 1 pound

GREECE
126.80 drachmas = U.S. $1
100 leptas = 1 drachma

JAPAN
250.20 yen = U.S. $1
100 sen = 1 yen

TURKEY
400 liras = U.S. $1
100 kurus = 1 lira

3 Reported speech: questions

TABLE 2

> ### TABLE 2:
> ### STATEMENTS ABOUT INTERNATIONAL CURRENCY
>
> They use Groschen and Schillings in Austria.
>
> There are 100 Groschen in a Schilling.
>
> 22.09 Schillings equals one U.S. dollar.
>
> You can get 22.09 Schillings for one dollar.
>
> The rate of exchange of Schillings to dollars is 22.09 to one.

C. Use the information in Tables 1 and 2 to complete these sentences. There are always several possible answers.

   Do you know *how many sen equal one Japanese yen?*

1. Can you tell me _____

2. Somebody asked me _____

3. Does anyone remember _____

4. I don't know _____

5. I wonder _____

6. Where can I find out _____

7. No one seems to know _____

Vocabulary Summary

bill	coin	dollar	quarter
cashier	conversion	equal	rate of exchange
cent	currency	exchange	wonder
change	dime	nickel	(be) worth

4 HOW and WHAT questions

Growing things

How is used to make information questions in three principal ways:

1. with adjectives, such as **long** and **far**.

   How long have you been growing roses?

2. with **much** (for costs and for general amounts) and **many**.

   How much are the tulip bulbs?
   How much topsoil will I need?
   How many kinds of palm tree are there?

3. alone, to talk about condition and method.

   How's your garden doing this year?
   How do you grow such beautiful roses?

How is also used with **come**, in informal speech, to ask for a reason:

   How come my ivy is dying?

What is used to make information questions in two principal ways:

1. with nouns, such as **time, color,** and **kind (of)**.

   What color are the tulips?

2. alone, as subject or object of the sentence.

   What are those things?
   What are you going to plant this spring?

What is also used with **for**, in informal speech, to ask for a reason:

   What did you pull up those plants for?

A. Write **How** or **What** in each blank.

   <u>How</u> many shrubs are you going to plant in front of your house?
1. _____ much time does it take to establish an asparagus bed?
2. _____ kinds of flower will grow in this climate?

4 How and WHAT questions   14

3. _____ tall will an oak tree grow?
4. _____'s your father spraying the garden for?
5. _____ are these bushes?
6. _____ big will this kind of lily get?
7. _____ colors do orchids come in?
8. _____ come you didn't plant any strawberries this year?
9. _____ old are your lilac bushes?
10. _____ time of the year is best for planting trees?
11. _____'s your flower bed this year?
12. _____ do you grow such beautiful squash?
13. _____ kind of seeds did you plant?
14. _____ much is the pink dogwood?
15. _____ variety of tree grows best here?

A.   B.   C.   D.

How many flowers can you name in English? A. _____
B. _____ C. _____ E. _____

B. Rearrange the words to form complete questions with **How** and **What**.

this   kind   of   what   is   plant
What kind of plant is this?

1. going you to many plant how are shrubs
   _____

2. this vegetable how's doing your year garden
   _____

3. you are doing that for what
   _____

4. have you come any don't how weeds your in garden
   _____

15   HOW and WHAT questions   4

5. here   I   plant   what   next   should   spring

   _____

6. climate   apple   in   what   do   trees   best   grow

   _____

7. how   time   usually   garden   you   in   much   spend   your   do

   _____

C. Write questions with **How** and **What**. Use information in the statements.

(I'm going to plant <u>roses</u> this year.)

What are you going to plant this year?

1. (The flowers are <u>99¢ a box</u>.)

2. (They're <u>lilies</u>.)

3. (This oak tree will be <u>sixty feet</u> tall.)

4. (We're putting <u>twelve</u> shrubs in front of our house.)

5. (It's <u>summer</u> squash.)

6. (It's a <u>pink</u> dogwood.)

7. (I prepared my garden <u>with fertilizer</u>.)

Vocabulary Summary

asparagus	garden	palm	strawberry
bed	grow	plant	topsoil
bulb	ivy	rose	tulip
bush	lilac	seed	variety
climate	lily	shrub	water
dogwood	oak	spray	weed
fertilizer	orchid	squash	

5 Compound sentences

Getting acquainted

Short additions with **but** always use a form of **be** or an auxiliary. If the first part of the sentence is affirmative, the auxiliary is negative. If the first part of the sentence is negative, the auxiliary is affirmative.

*Consuelo **is** from Colombia. Chang **isn't** from Colombia.*
*Consuelo **is** from Colombia, **but** Chang **isn't**.*
*Chang **isn't** from Colombia, **but** Consuelo **is**.*

Sentences connected by **and** may be affirmative or negative.

1. **Too** is affirmative.

   *Ashraf **studied** English in high school. Hoa Thi **studied** English in high school.*
   *Ashraf **studied** English in high school, **and** Hoa Thi **did, too**.*

2. **Either** is negative.

   *Olga **doesn't like** grammar. Julius **doesn't like** grammar.*
   *Olga **doesn't like** grammar, **and** Julius **doesn't either**.*

3. **So** (affirmative) and **neither** (negative) have the same meaning and function as **too** and **either**, but the word order changes.

                         S   V
   *Ashraf studied English in high school, and **Hoa Thi did too**.*

                         V   S
   *Ashraf studied English in high school, and **so did Hoa Thi**.*

                         S   V
   *Olga doesn't like grammar, and **Julius doesn't either**.*

                         V   S
   *Olga doesn't like grammar, and **neither does Julius**.*

5 Compound sentences: short additions

> Especially in conversation, the clauses with **too, so, either,** and **neither** are often used as sentences by themselves.
>
> *Where are you from?*
> *Colombia.*
> *I am too! / So am I!*
> *I didn't like English at first, but now I do.*
> *I didn't either. / Neither did I.*

At the first meeting of an ESL class, the students are getting acquainted. Each student asks another these questions:

1. **What's your name?**
2. **Where are you from?**
3. **Do you live with your family?**
4. **How many languages can you speak?**
5. **How long have you studied English?**

The teacher puts the responses on the board like this:

Question #1	#2	#3	#4	#5
Consuelo (f)	Colombia	no	2	2 years
Ricardo (m)	Mexico	no	2	3 years
Chang (m)	Korea	yes	2	1 year
Walther (m)	Germany	no	5	2 years
Athanasios (m)	Greece	yes	3	1 year
Ashraf (f)	Iran	yes	3	3 years
Hoa Thi (f)	Vietnam	yes	2	2 years
Julius (m)	Indonesia	no	3	3 years
Olga (f)	Colombia	no	2	1 year

f = female   m = male

5 Compound sentences: short additions 18

Use the information on the chart to write exercises A, B, and C. Some possible answers are given in the answer section.

A. Write sentences with **but** and short additions.

Consuelo is from Colombia, but Ricardo isn't.

1. ___
2. ___
3. ___
4. ___
5. ___
6. ___
7. ___
8. ___
9. ___
10. ___

B. Write pairs of affirmative sentences, one with **too** and one with **so**.

a. *Chang lives with his family, and Athanasios does too.*
b. *Chang lives with his family, and so does Athanasios.*

1. a. ___
   b. ___
2. a. ___
   b. ___
3. a. ___
   b. ___
4. a. ___
   b. ___
5. a. ___
   b. ___
6. a. ___
   b. ___
7. a. ___
   b. ___
8. a. ___
   b. ___

19 Compound sentences: short additions 5

C. Write pairs of negative sentences, one with **either** and one with **neither**.

   a. <u>Hoa Thi hasn't studied English for three years, and Olga hasn't either.</u>
   b. <u>Hoa Thi hasn't studied English for three years, and neither has Olga.</u>

1. a. _____
   b. _____
2. a. _____
   b. _____
3. a. _____
   b. _____
4. a. _____
   b. _____
5. a. _____
   b. _____
6. a. _____
   b. _____
7. a. _____
   b. _____
8. a. _____
   b. _____
9. a. _____
   b. _____
10. a. _____
    b. _____

6 Review of tag questions

Around the world in 67 days

> We <u>use</u> tag questions in conversation to get confirmation of an idea we already have.
>
> *You saw the Great Wall of China on your trip, didn't you? (I think you saw the Great Wall. Am I right?)*
> *Yes, I did. (Yes, you're right.)*
>
> We <u>form</u> tag questions in two ways:
>
> 1. affirmative statement (+), negative tag (−) for an expected affirmative answer (+)*
>
>   *It was your first time in China, wasn't it?*
>   *Yes, it was.*
>
> 2. negative statement (−), affirmative tag (+) for an expected negative answer (−)*
>
>   *You weren't disappointed, were you?*
>   *No, I certainly wasn't.*
>
> *The answer is sometimes not the expected one:
>
>   *You would go again, wouldn't you?*
>   *I don't think so, no.*
>
> When you form tag questions, remember:
> 1. The tag consists of a verb and **it, there**, or a pronoun,
> 2. The verb in the tag is either a form of **be** or an auxiliary. If the verb in the statement has more than one auxiliary, use only the first auxiliary in the tag.
>
>   *You **hadn't been planning on** going to China originally, **had** you?*
>
> 3. The pronoun in the tag refers to the subject of the statement. Use **it** for all impersonal noun and pronoun subjects, including gerunds, **today, this,** etc.
>
>   ***Standing** on the Great Wall was a thrill, wasn't **it**?*

Two people are discussing the trip around the world that one of them has just taken. In their conversation, change each "I think" or "I don't think" statement to a tag question.

Fritz: I don't think you've been back very long.
You haven't been back very long, have you?

21 Review of tag questions 6

Manny: No, I just got back Tuesday.
Fritz: I think you were away for two months.

Manny: Exactly sixty-seven days.
Fritz: I think the trip was exciting.

Manny: It certainly was.
Fritz: I think you're exhausted now, though.

Manny: Not really. I took it pretty easy.
Fritz: Well, tell me all about it. I think you went to New York first.

Manny: Yes. I don't think you've been there.

Fritz: No, but of course I've heard a lot about it. I don't think you got mugged there.

Manny: I think you think it's a dangerous place.

Fritz: Well, yes.
Manny: I had no problem whatsoever. And everyone was friendly.
Fritz: I think that's surprising.

Manny: Not really. I think people usually treat you the way you treat them.

Fritz: You're right. What did you like best about New York?
Manny: The shows. I especially liked "A Chorus Line."
Fritz: I think that's their longest-running musical.

Manny: Right.
Fritz: I think you went to San Francisco from New York.

Manny: Uh-huh.
Fritz: I think that's where they have those cable cars.

I don't think they were running while you were there, though.

6 Review of tag questions 22

I think they were being repaired then.

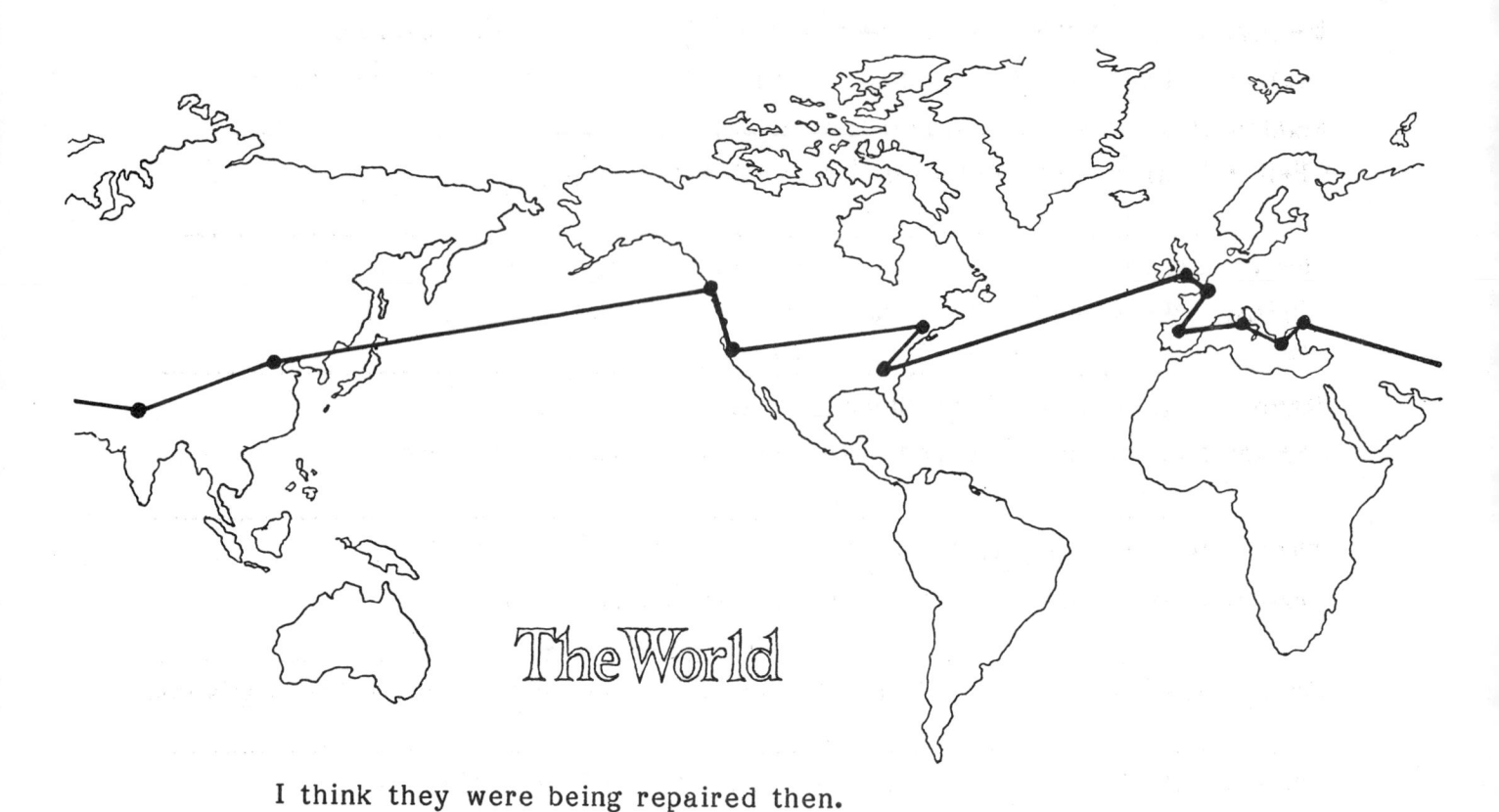

Manny: No, they'd just gone back into operation. They're quite exciting -- especially going downhill.
Fritz: I don't think you expect to be able to stop.

Manny: Right, but you always do.
Fritz: Where did you go after San Francisco?
Manny: To Vancouver, for my flight to China.
Fritz: I think you saw the Great Wall.

I think that it was built over 2,000 years ago.

Manny: Mostly, but it wasn't finished until about 1600.
Fritz: Did you go to Beijing?
Manny: Yes, but for only two days, unfortunately.
Fritz: I think you would have liked to stay longer.

Manny: Certainly. But we went on to Agra, India.
Fritz: I think that's where the Taj Mahal is.

Review of tag questions 6

Manny: Yes, and it's even more beautiful than it looks in pictures.
Fritz: I should imagine. I hope to get there someday. What was next?
Manny: Next was a long flight to Istanbul.
Fritz: I think that used to be called Constantinople.

___

Manny: That's right. The Topkapi Palace was especially fascinating.
Fritz: I think there was a movie made about that.

___

Manny: Well, it took place there, anyway.
Fritz: I don't think you can take the Orient Express anymore.

___

Manny: Not from Istanbul, no. I flew from there to Athens.
Fritz: I don't think you spent all your time in Athens.

___

Manny: Yes, I did. I think I should have taken a cruise around the Greek islands.

___

Fritz: I think so. I think this was your trip, not mine, though.

___

Manny: True. I think you've been thinking about a cruise around the islands.

___

Fritz: Yes, I have. I'm hoping to go this winter. I don't think you came directly from Athens to London.

___

Manny: No, I stopped off in Rome and Paris.
Fritz: That's wonderful. I think traveling is broadening.

___

Manny: Indeed it is. I gained more than 15 pounds

Vocabulary Summary

(be) back	exhausted	island	tell about
broadening	fascinating	long-running	thrill
cable car	(be) (one's)	musical (n.)	trip
cruise	first time	show (n.)	
dangerous	flight	spend time	
directly	get back	stop off	
disappointed	go (back) into	surprising	
downhill	operation	take it easy	
exciting	hear about	take place	

7 Agent suffixes

Occupations

> Note the agent suffixes:
>
> 1. Someone who { farms / sails } is { a farm**er**. / a sail**or**. }
>
> The root word (**farm, sail**) is not always an English verb: for example, **carpent**er, **plumb**er, **doct**or, and **janit**or.
> The **-er** and **-or** suffixes can indicate things, as well as people: for example, comput**er**, dry**er**, elevat**or**, and refrigerat**or**.
>
> 2. Someone who specializes in { music / geology } is { a musici**an**. / a geolog**ist**. }
>
> The **-an** suffix is often preceded by **-ci-**.
> The **-ist** suffix is used for the players of many musical instruments: clarinet**ist**, harp**ist**, organ**ist**, etc.

A. Fill each blank with a word ending in **-er** or **-or**.

Abel makes announcements on TV. He's a TV _announcer_.

1. Benjamin designs clothing for women. He's a clothes _____.
2. Carol directs plays and her husband produces them. She's a _____, and he's a _____.
3. Daisy operates and programs a computer. She's a computer _____ and _____.
4. Everyone in Eliana's family is in the arts. Her mother sculpts, her father dances, her brother sings, and Eliana paints. Eliana is a _____. Her mother is a _____, her father is a _____, and her brother is a _____.
5. Francisco reports and comments on politics for the daily newspaper. He's a newspaper _____, and _____.
6. Glenda works in education at a local high school. She's a member of the administration and counsels troubled students. Glenda is an _____, an _____, and a _____.

25   Agent suffixes 7

7. Hayashi edits and publishes books about career opportunities. He's an _____ and _____.

B. Fill in each blank with a word ending in **-cian**.

Inigo specializes in music. He's a _musician_.

1. Jerry makes electrical repairs on small appliances. He works as an _____.
2. Kay works in a beauty salon. She's a _____.
3. Luz studied technical aspects of giving X-rays. She's now a trained X-ray _____.
4. Muhammed works at a small clinic that does phsychological testing. He's a _____.
5. Nora prepares special diets for the residents of a nursing home. She's a _____.
6. Omar has specialized in mathematics. He's a _____.
7. Peder is an expert in statistics. He's a _____.

C. Complete the chart with the necessary articles and words ending in **-ist**.

Someone who specializes in

	archeology	is an _archeologist_.
1.	dental hygiene	is a dental _____.
2.	physics	is a _____.
3.	journalism	is a _____.
4.	biology	is a _____.
5.	chemistry	is a _____.
6.	psychology	is a _____.
7.	physical therapy	is a physical _____.
8.	cardiology	is a _____.
9.	hypnotism	is a _____.

D. From the box, choose the name of the profession for each blank.

aviator	florist	physician
barber	janitor	pianist
dentist	optician	teller
	pharmacist	

7 Agent suffixes   26

Quentin is a concert *pianist*. He studied at the Eastman School of Music, specializing in the works of Chopin.

1. Rama is a _____ who specializes in root canal work. He's married to his hygienist.

2. Salome fills doctor's prescriptions at the drug store on the corner where she's a _____.

3. Titus was an _____ during World War I. He's decided that he's too old for flying now.

4. Ursula got her M.D. at the University of Basel. She's a _____ whose specialization is oncology.

5. Vivian fits people with new eyeglasses. She's an _____.

6. Werner, my _____, gives the best haircuts in town.

7. Xerxes is a _____ at the West Middle School. He cleans the classrooms at night after everyone has gone home.

8. Yolanda hopes to become a bank manager someday. She started her job as a _____ last week.

9. Zena is a _____. She spent all day yesterday making arrangements of roses and daisies for the Mother's Day rush this weekend.

Vocabulary Summary

administrator	dentist	job	politician
announcer	designer	journalist	producer
archeologist	dietician	mathematician	programmer
aviator	director	musician	psychologist
barber	doctor	novelist	publisher
beautician	editor	occupation	reporter
biologist	educator	operator	sailor
cardiologist	electrician	optician	sculptor
career	expert	organist	singer
carpenter	farmer	painter	specialization
chemist	florist	pharmacist	specialize
clinician	geologist	physician	statistician
commentator	hygienist	physicist	technician
counselor	hypnotist	pianist	teller
dancer	janitor	plumber	therapist

Abstract nouns 8

Quotations

> Some abstract nouns are non-count and so are not used in the plural. These include the names for ideas, fields of study, and sports: for example, **integration, chemistry,** and **golf**.
>
> Others may be count or non-count, depending upon their meaning. When used in a countable sense, they refer to individuals in a group, may take an article or a plural, and have the meaning of "a form/forms of":
>
> *"Two **loves** (forms of love) I have of comfort and despair."*
> (William Shakespeare)
>
> When used in a non-countable sense, they refer to the whole abstract idea, take no plural, and are used without **a, an,** or **the** unless followed by a qualifying phrase or clause.
>
> *"'Oh, 'tis **love**, 'tis **love**, that makes the world go round!'"*
> (Lewis Carroll)
>
> *"I love thee with **a love** I seemed to lose*
> *With my lost saints...."*
> (Elizabeth Barrett Browning)

A. Can these nouns take a plural? Answer **yes** or **no**.

_____ 1. sacrifice   _____ 11. comfort
_____ 2. knowledge   _____ 12. willingness
_____ 3. decision   _____ 13. service
_____ 4. triumph   _____ 14. labor
_____ 5. information   _____ 15. worship
_____ 6. friendship   _____ 16. work
_____ 7. appreciation   _____ 17. adoration
_____ 8. desire   _____ 18. popularity
_____ 9. laughter   _____ 19. merriment
_____ 10. sincerity   _____ 20. life

8 Abstract nouns

B. Fill each blank with an article or an **x** (no article possible).

1. "____ great end of ____ life is not ____ knowledge but ____ action." (**T. H. Huxley**)
2. "____ liberty cannot be preserved without ____ general knowledge among ____ people." (**John Adams**)
3. "____ thought makes ____ whole dignity of ____ man." (**Pascal**)
4. "____ discontent is ____ first step in ____ progress of ____ man or ____ nation." (**Oscar Wilde**)
5. "____ love of ____ money is ____ root of all ____ evil." (**The Bible**)
6. "____ progress is ____ law of ____ life; ____ man is not ____ man as yet." (**Robert Browning**)
7. "____ first requisite for... ____ happiness is ____ abolition of ____ religion." (**Marx**)
8. "No personal consideration should stand in the way of performing ____ public duty." (**U. S. Grant**)
9. "____ business of ____ samurai consists in ... devoting himself to ____ duty above all." (**Yamaga Soko**)

Abstract nouns 8

10. "_____ experience is _____ father of _____ wisdom." (**Anonymous**)
11. "_____ world fears _____ new experience more than it fears anything." (**D. H. Lawrence**)
12. "_____ marriage...is _____ damnably serious business, particularly around Boston." (**J. P. Marquand**)
13. "_____ business of America is _____ business." (**Calvin Coolidge**)
14. "_____ liberty like _____ charity must begin at _____ home." (**J. B. Conant**)
15. "_____ goal of all _____ life is _____ death." (**Freud**)
16. "_____ single death is _____ tragedy, _____ million deaths is _____ statistic." (**Stalin**)
17. "_____ human misery is too great for _____ men to do without _____ faith." (**Heine**)
18. "_____ education is _____ life itself." (**John Dewey**)
19. "_____ foundation of every state is _____ education of its youth." (**Diogenes**)
20. "Lack of _____ money is _____ root of all _____ evil." (**George Bernard Shaw**)
21. "He is _____ best of _____ men who dislikes _____ power." (**Mohammed**)
22. "_____ greater _____ powers, _____ more dangerous _____ abuse." (**Edmund Burke**)
23. "_____ nations have been born in _____ war and expired in _____ peace." (**Yates Sterling**)
24. "There never was _____ good war or _____ bad peace." (**Benjamin Franklin**)
25. "When _____ power leads _____ man toward _____ arrogance, _____ poetry reminds him of his limitations." (**John F. Kennedy**)

Vocabulary Summary

abuse	discontent	law	religion
action	duty	liberty	sacrifice
adoration	education	life	service
appreciation	evil	love	sincerity
arrogance	experience	marriage	thought
business	faith	merriment	tragedy
charity	friendship	misery	triumph
comfort	happiness	money	war
death	information	peace	willingness
decision	integration	poetry	wisdom
desire	knowledge	popularity	work
despair	labor	power	worship
dignity	laughter	progress	

9 -SELF/SELVES pronouns

Social relations

The **-self/-selves** pronouns are:

myself	ourselves
yourself	yourselves
himself*	themselves
herself*	
itself*	
oneself**	

* In careful speech and writing, use **himself** when the reference is indefinite:

*There would be little social progress if **each person** cared only about **himself**.*

** **One** and **oneself** are used impersonally in formal speech and writing:

*Despite some philosophers' advice, it is very difficult for **one** to know **oneself**.*

These pronouns are used **reflexively** with certain verbs and adjectives:

***People** would get along better if **they** could see **themselves** as others see them. What do **you** do when you feel **ashamed of yourself** for something you've done?*

They are used **intensively** for emphasis:

***Yacoub himself** is his own worst critic.*

With **by**, a **-self/-selves** pronoun means **alone, without help**:

*Helene always tries to work out her problems **by herself**.*

Fill in each blank with an appropriate **-self/-selves** pronoun.

1. You have to learn to assert _____. Stand up for _____. No one else is going to fight your battles for you. They're too busy looking out for _____.
2. Although I think it's important for everyone to like _____ before he can really like others, sometimes I don't like _____ very much.
3. Sigmund Freud _____ said that in everything we do, we are serving _____.

-SELF/-SELVES pronouns

4. Do you really listen to other people during a conversation, or are you thinking about what you _____ are going to say next?

5. President Franklin Delano Roosevelt said, "The only thing we have to fear is fear _____."

6. Did Benjamin Franklin say, "God helps them that help _____."?

7. When my wife and I visited friends in the United States, our hostes told us, "Make _____ at home." Did she _____ realize what she was saying? What if we had taken her literally?

8. If someone hurts his feelings, Leonardo keeps his reaction to _____.

9. Florinda is proud of _____ because she's very beautiful. She forgets that we can't give _____ either credit or blame for genetic accidents. Those result from birth _____, not from anything we _____ have accomplished.

10. I consider _____ to be altruistic, but people like Albert Bandura say, "All of you who think you're helping others are really just making _____ feel better. You're afraid that if you don't help others, they'll treat you less kindly."

11. The person who says to you, "I like being by _____" may be fooling _____.

12. According to the Epicurean philosophy, you should enjoy _____ today, for you never know what will happen tomorrow.

Vocabulary Summary

admit	credit	kindly	reaction
agreeable	critic	look out for	relations
altrusitic	discussion	(take care of)	social
ashamed (of)	feelings	problem	stand up for
assert	fool	progress	unpleasant
behavior	get along	proud (of)	work out (solve)
blame	(be congenial)	punish	

10 Impersonal pronouns

Driving

> The following pronouns are often used impersonally, to make generalizations: **we, you, they,** and **one** (formal). Used this way, the pronouns have no specific antecedents, but mean "a person or people in general."
>
> *We have to remember that driving is a privilege, not a right.*
> *You're not allowed to drive over 55 on any highway in the U.S.*
> *In 1835, they passed a drive-on-the-right law in New Jersey.*
> *One has to learn to drive one's (his/her) car defensively at all times.*

A. Fill in each blank with either **you** or **they**.

1. Hal: Jerry, I still have my Nebraska driver's license. Where do ____ have to go to get one in Connecticut?
   Jerry: Well, Hal, ____ have two offices about the same distance from here. ____ can go to either Enfield or Wethersfield.
   Hal: Will ____ make me take a road test or a written test? Or can I just transfer my license?
   Jerry: ____'ll probably give you a written test.
   Hal: Do you know what ____ charge?
   Jerry: Gee, I don't remember, it's been so long since I got mine.

2. Jill: Motor Vehicle Department. Can I help you?
   Hal: What do ____ have to do to get a Connecticut driver's license? I have a valid one from Nebraska.
   Jill: ____ have to report to this office or one of the others and fill out the forms.
   Hal: Will I have to take a test?
   Jill: That depends, sir. ____'ll tell you after you get here and fill out the forms.
   Hal: How do ____ get there from downtown Hartford?
   Jill: ____ take 91 south, get off at exit 43, and follow the signs.
   Hal: Thank you.

Impersonal pronouns 10

B. These are some obligations of a courteous driver. Restate them with **We** and **should** or **shouldn't**.

Dim your lights when you approach another vehicle.
We should dim our lights when we approach another vehicle.

1. Don't honk your horn unnecessarily.

2. Give pedestrians the right of way.

3. Don't forget to signal when you're changing lanes.

4. Always be careful to part between the marked lines in a parking lot. Don't take up more than one space.

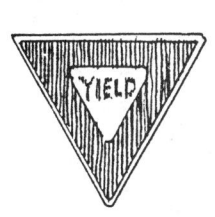

C. These are some laws about driving in the State of Connecticut. Restate them formally and firmly with **One** and **must** or **must not**. Make other necessary changes.

Be at least sixteen years old to learn to drive.
One must be at least sixteen years old to learn to drive.

1. Come to a complete stop at a stop sign.

2. Do not park within ten feet of a fire hydrant.

3. Do not exceed the speed limit.

4. Present your car for inspection if it is ten or more years old.

10 Impersonal pronouns 34

D. Mark each underlined pronoun as specific **(S)** or general **(G)** (impersonal).

What time do <u>they</u>(G) open at the Department of Motor Vehicles, do <u>you</u>(S) know?

1. I saw the first stop sign all right, but I didn't see the second <u>one</u> at all.
2. Don't <u>you</u> think <u>we</u> should buy a new car, dear?
3. <u>You</u> have to be especially careful driving on Friday and Saturday nights. <u>They</u> say that's when most accidents happen.
4. <u>One</u> must not have a police radar detector in Connecticut.
5. The Johnsons told me <u>they</u> don't have any insurance. I thought <u>you</u> had to have it to drive here.
6. Can <u>you</u> tell me whether <u>we</u> can turn right on a red light in this state?
7. Would <u>you</u> mind slowing down? <u>We</u> have speed limits for a reason, <u>you</u> know.

Vocabulary Summary

accident	fire hydrant	lane	signal
approach	form (document)	law	speed limit
defensively	highway	park	take up (occupy)
dim	honk	pedestrian	transfer
driver's license	horn	privilege	valid
exceed	inspection	radar detector	vehicle
fill out	insurance	right of way	

Indefinite compound pronouns 11

Fear, jealousy, and suspicion

We form indefinite compound pronouns by combining **some, any, no,** and **every** with **-one**/**-body** or **-thing**:

    someone/somebody   no one/nobody
    something   nothing

    anyone/anybody   everyone/everybody
    anything   everything

The compounds with **-body** are more informal than those with **-one**.

We use indefinite compound pronouns in these ways:

1. compounds with **some** in affirmative statements and in questions.

    *There's **something** I must tell you.*
    *Uh-oh. Is it **something** I want to hear?*

2. compounds with (**not**) **any** and **no** in negative statements and in questions.

    *Isn't there **anyone** who can help me? / Is there **no one** who can help me?*
    *No, **not anyone**. / No, **no one**.*

3. compounds with **every** in both statements and questions.

    *I'm afraid **everybody** in the neighborhood heard our argument.*
    ***Not everybody**. The Cheltons are away in Florida.*

All of these pronouns are singular. In informal usage, however, following plural pronouns are increasingly accepted:

    ***Somebody** left **their** (formally, **his**) footprints in the snow under my window.*

Indefinite compound pronouns are often followed by adjectives or by **else**.

    *I have something **important** to tell you.*
    *Oh no. Is there someone **else**?*

11 Indefinite compound pronouns 36

Fill in each blank with an indefinite compound pronoun. Some will have more than one possible answer.

1. Gladys: There's _____ waving to you from across the room. Who is she, _____ you know?

   Marcel: No, it's _____ I recognize, but I'll wave back anyway. Hello!

   Gladys: You know, I've noticed _____ interesting about you. Everywhere we go, _____ seems to know you, but you don't recognize _____.

   Marcel: Don't be jealous. Don't you know that I love _____ but you?

   Gladys: I'm so confused that I don't know _____ anymore.

   Marcel: But I always tell you _____.

   Gladys: _____?

   Marcel: Well, maybe not _____. Do you want to know _____ right now? The reason I don't recognize _____ is that I'm terribly nearsighted, and I'm too vain to wear glasses.

   Gladys: That's interesting, but it still doesn't explain why all those women know you.

Indefinite compound pronouns 11

2. Marilyn: Ah, there's _____ like getting home after a long trip. _____ ever told me three weeks away could seem so long. I can't wait to get _____ unpacked and settle in again.

   Joe: There's the house at last. Looks good, doesn't it?

   Marilyn: Wait, _____'s wrong. The front door is open.

   Joe: Oh no. Do you think there's _____ inside?

   Marilyn: We'd better find out. Stick with me....Hello? Is _____ there?....Listen. Do you hear _____?

   Joe: No.

   Marilyn: Neither do I, but let's be careful.

   Joe: I haven't found _____ missing, have you?

   Marilyn: No, _____ seems to be O.K. What a relief I wonder why the door was open, though. Do you suppose we left it like that?

   Joe: It's possible. It's amazing that _____ noticed it, with all the traffic going by here...

   Marilyn: Ssssh. I think I just heard _____ moving around in the cellar.

Vocabulary Summary

amazing	footprint	notice	wave (a hand)
arguement	jealous	recognize	
confused	jealousy	relief	
fear	missing	suspicion	

12 Quantity words with partitives I

A picnic

Quantity words followed by **of** phrases specify parts of a group.

1. Quantity words may be cardinal numbers.

    A: *This is **one** of the best picnics we've ever had.*
    B: *It's almost the only picnic we've had. Remember, **four** of them have been rained out!*

2. Quantity words may substitute for specific names, numbers, or amounts.

    Everybody who came to the picnic brought dessert, so we had four pies and two chocolate cakes. The pies were peach, cherry, strawberry, and rhubarb.
    ***All** of the people who came to the picnic brought dessert.*
    ***None** (not any) of the pies were pumpkin.*
    ***Both** of the cakes were chocolate.*
    ***Neither** (not either) of the cakes was really delicious.*

Both and **neither** are used with plural count nouns. In formal speech and writing, **neither** is singular, but plural verbs are common in informal conversation:

   ***Neither** of the cakes was (were) very good.*

All and **none** are used with plural count nouns and with non-count nouns. Whether they are singular or plural depends on the object of the preposition **of**:

   ***All** of the **pies were** delicious. (count)*
   ***All** of the **fruit** in them **was** fresh. (non-count)*
   ***None** of the **pies were** terrible.*
   ***None** of the **fruit** in them **was** canned.*

3. The words **one(s), another,** and **the other(s)**, without an **of** phrase, may substitute for count nouns.

    *One of the pies was peach. **Another (one)** was cherry. **The others (The other ones)** were strawberry and rhubarb. One of the cakes was chocolate. So was **the other (one)**.*

For additional quantity words used with partitives, see Lesson 13.

Quantity words with partitives I 12

A. Fill in the blanks with **all, none, not any, both, neither,** or **not either.**

1. Paul: Is _not any_ of the peach pie left?
   Sally: Not a crumb. In fact, _____ of the pies are completely gone.
2. Paul: _____ of these two potato salads look right to me. Don't they look a little greenish?
   Sally: We'd better _____ eat _____ of them.
3. Paul: Are _____ _____ of the hot dogs ready yet? I'm starving
   Sally: No, _____ of them are ready. _____ of them need a few more minutes to cook -- unless you like them raw.
   Paul: No, thanks. I'll wait.
4. Paul: Didn't you and Glenna enjoy the picnic? _____ of you look a little unhappy.
   Sally: Well, _____ of us wanted to say anything to spoil other people's good time, but _____ of the food was much to write home about, and we were _____ interested in _____ of the games, either. Maybe _____ of us were just tired. _____ of the kids have been sick this week.
   Paul: All four of them? You must be exhausted!

B. Circle the correct verb. All are used in informal conversation.

1. Glenna: Neither of the cakes (was, were) anything to write home about.
   Sally: No, but all of the pies (was, were) excellent. I know. I had a slice of each.
2. Glenna: (Isn't, Aren't) either of you going to the next picnic, on the Fourth?
   Sally: I'm afraid both of us (is, are) going to be away.

12   Quantity words withs partitives I

3. Glenna: When do we eat? I'm starving.
   Sally: It'll be a little while. None of the soda (is, are) cold yet, and none of the hamburgers (is, are) cooked.
   Glenna: Need some help?
4. Glenna: (Is, Are) all of the potato salad gone already?
   Sally: No, none of it (was, were) fit to eat. It had gone bad, probably from being in the sun too long.
5. Glenna: How come both of you (is, are) sitting here? Don't you know there's a ball game going on?
   Sally: Yeah, but neither of us (knows, know) how to play.
   Glenna: Don't worry about it. None of us (plays, play) very well either.

C. Fill in the blanks with **one, ones, another, the other,** or **the others.**

1. During the summer, there are three major holidays when Americans often have picnics. One is Memorial Day, May 30. _____ is the Fourth of July. _____ is Labor Day.
2. If you don't like that salad, try this _____. I think it's better than _____, even though it isn't very good. Too bad nobody brought _____.
3. Some of the kids are playing baseball. Heaven knows what _____ are doing.
4. Who wants _____ can of soda? There's plenty. _____ are cooling in the lake. Nobody wants to drink warm _____.
5. I found one of the kids, but I still haven't seen any of _____. This _____ either doesn't know or isn't telling where _____ are.

Vocabulary Summary

cake	dessert	hot dog	(be) rained out
can (n.)	(be) fit	(be) left	raw
canned	fresh	peach	rhubarb
cherry	fruit	picnic	slice
chocolate	go bad	pie	soda
crumb	hamburger	potato salad	starving
delicious	holiday	pumpkin	strawberry

Quantity words with partitives II

Pleasure and satisfaction

Quantity words followed by **of** phrases distinguish parts of a group. These quantity words are less specific than the ones in Lesson 12. They are used with plural count nouns and with non-count nouns, with some important differences.

with plural count nouns	largest number or amount	with non-count nouns
a lot/lots	↑	a lot/lots
many		much
quite a few		quite a bit
some, any		some, any
several		
	↓	
a few/not many	smallest number or amount	a little/not much
few		little

Use **many, much,** and **any** in negative statements and in questions. (**Many** and **much** are used in affirmative statements in more formal conversation and writing.) Use **quite a few, quite a bit,** and **some** in affirmative statements and in questions.

Few and **little** emphasize the smallness of the number or amount.

Hobbies of a Sampling of 100 Students

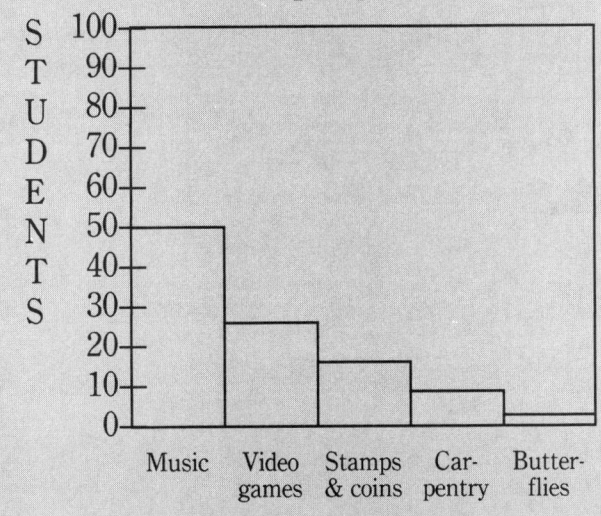

A lot/Lots/Quite a few of the students enjoy music.

Some of them like video games.

Several of them collect stamps and coins.

A few/Not many of them enjoy carpentry.

Very *few of* them collect butterflies.

13 Quantity words with partitives II

Average Amount of Money Spent on Hobbies Per Month

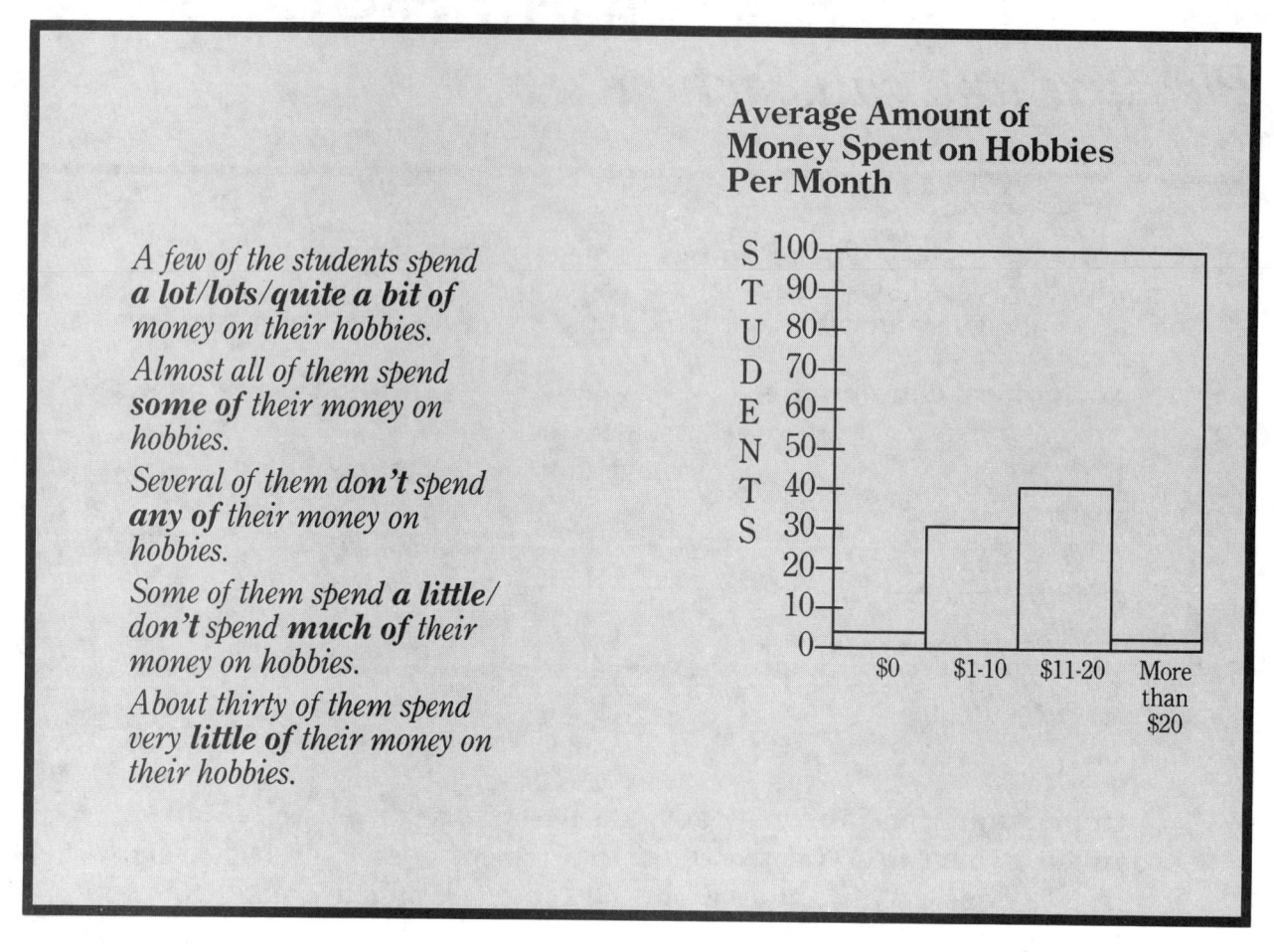

*A few of the students spend **a lot/lots/quite a bit of** money on their hobbies.*

*Almost all of them spend **some of** their money on hobbies.*

*Several of them **don't** spend **any of** their money on hobbies.*

*Some of them spend **a little/** don't spend **much of** their money on hobbies.*

*About thirty of them spend very **little of** their money on their hobbies.*

A. These are the **results of a survey** in which people were asked what kind of reading they enjoy most.

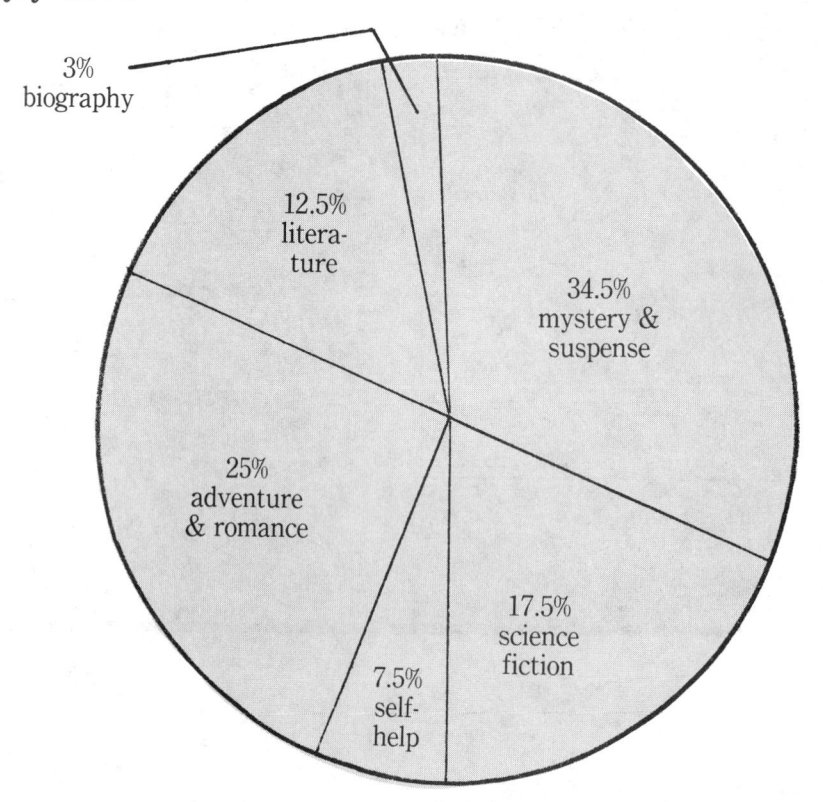

- 3% biography
- 12.5% literature
- 34.5% mystery & suspense
- 25% adventure & romance
- 7.5% self-help
- 17.5% science fiction

Quantity words with partitives II   13

Using information from the graph, write sentences that contain quantity words with partitives.

Some of the people surveyed said they enjoy reading science fiction the most.

1. _____
2. _____
3. _____
4. _____
5. _____
6. _____

B. Another group of people were asked how much of their enjoyment, on a scale of 0 - 5, they get from reading. These are the results.

RATING	PERCENTAGE
0	5%
1	8%
2	19%
3	36%
4	17%
5	15%

13 Quantity words with partitives II

Write sentences using quantity words with partitives.

36% said they get some of their enjoyment from reading.

1.
2.
3.
4.
5.
6.

C. Fill in the blanks with **quite a few of** or **quite a bit of**.

Quite a few of my friends enjoy collecting butterflies as much as I do.

1. I get _____ my enjoyment from carpentry.
2. It's true that one can get _____ satisfaction from helping others.
3. We spent _____ our vacation relaxing on the beach.
4. Were there _____ your relatives at the family reunion?
5. Haven't you been getting _____ pleasure from your new hobby?

Quantity words with partitives II

D. Fill in the blanks with **many** or **much**.

1. **Tammy:** I'm lucky. I don't have _____ of the problems most people seem to have.
   Rocky: That may be so, but _____ of anyone's "luck" depends on the person more than the circumstances.
2. **Tammy:** Don't you agree that _____ of life's pleasures become even more enjoyable with age?
   Rocky: I'm not sure. Not _____ of my pleasure seems to come from playing cricket anymore.
3. **Tammy:** You don't seem to spend _____ of your money on your hobbies.
   Rocky: That's because _____ of the things I like are free.

E. Fill in the blanks with **few** or **little**.

1. **Tammy:** _____ of the people I know know as much about life as you do. Do you do a lot of reading?
   Rocky: No, very _____ of my knowledge comes from books. It really just comes from living itself.
2. **Tammy:** A _____ of us are going out for dinner tonight. Would you like to come?
   Rocky: I'm not sure I can afford it, but I would if you're having Chinese food. A _____ of that goes a long way.
3. **Tammy:** Marriage must agree with you. You look wonderful
   Rocky: <u>Marriage</u> is wonderful. When I was single, I had a lot of problems, especially loneliness. Now I have _____ of the loneliness, and _____ of the other problems as well.

Vocabulary Summary

adventure	hobby	pleasure	self-help
biography	knowledge	relax	suspense
collect	literature	reunion	vacation
enjoy	luck(y)	romance	
enjoyable	marriage	satisfaction	
enjoyment	mystery	science fiction	

14 Anticipatory It

New York City

The anticipatory **it** fills the usual subject position, but is not the true subject. It makes sentences more informal by displacing other constructions, which are generally used only in formal writing:

1. a subject noun clause

   That New York is one of the world's most exciting cities is common knowledge.
   *It's common knowledge **that New York is one of the world's most exciting cities.***

   Note: In informal conversation, **it** and the verb are almost always contracted.

2. a subject infinitive phrase

   ***To go there** has been one of my life's dreams.*
   *It's been one of my life's dreams **to go there.***

A common use of the anticipatory **it** is with a form of **take** + an infinitive, to describe the length of time or amount of effort necessary to complete an action:

*How long **does it take** to get used to New York?*
***It took** everything we'd saved to pay for our trip, but it was worth it.*

A. Rewrite these sentences with **it** displacing the subject noun clause.

That everyone wants to visit New York is common knowledge.
It's common knowledge that everyone wants to visit New York.

1. That you shouldn't expect to see everything in a few days is apparent, though.
   _____
   _____

2. That there are almost infinite numbers of things to do in the city is a fact.
   _____
   _____

Anticipatory It 14

3. That you get around as much as possible on foot would be advisable, because transportation is expensive.

4. That New Yorkers are always uncooperative is a common perception.

5. That they can be hospitable has often surprised visitors.

6. However, that the pace of life in New York is faster than it is almost anywhere else in the world seems to be true.

7. That a visit to New York will be an unforgettable adventure can fairly be said.

B. Rewrite these sentences with *it* displacing the subject infinitive phrases.

To spend much time in New York can be hazardous to your health.
It can be hazardous to your health to spend much time in New York.

1. On the other hand, to discover its wonders can be exciting.

2. To take packaged tours may be more convenient.

3. To spend a great deal of money isn't necessary.

4. For example, to buy half-price theater tickets at the kiosk at Broadway and 46th Street will save you money.

14 Anticipatory IT 48

5. And to go to the top of the RCA Building, the Empire State Building, or the World Trade Center for the fabulous views doesn't cost much.
   _____
   _____

6. To find your way around the city isn't hard.
   _____
   _____

7. To avoid subways might be wise.
   _____
   _____

C. Fill in the blanks with **it** and a form of **take**.

Chan: Have you ever accustomed yourself to New York's hustle and bustle? How long did _____ _____?

Juan: _____ can _____ a while. I'd say that _____ _____ me about a year after I moved here to feel really relaxed most of the time.

Chan: Has _____ _____ a lot of energy and effort?

Juan: Sure. That's why I'm relaxed. I'm too exhausted to be tense.

Chan: How much money does _____ _____ to live here comfortably?

Juan: _____ _____ more than I can earn. _____ will probably _____ me several more years to get my income to match my expenses.

D. Using the information on the chart, write short conversations with <u>it take(s)</u>. Assume an average driving speed of 50 miles per hour.

Distances in Miles Between Some U.S. Cities

	Atlanta	Chicago	Dallas	Los Angeles	Miami	New York	Seattle	Washington
Atlanta GA	----	708	822	2191	663	854	2625	618
Chicago IL	708	----	921	2048	1397	809	2052	709
Dallas TX	822	921	----	1399	1343	1559	2131	1307
Los Angeles CA	2191	2048	1399	----	2716	2794	1134	2646
Miami FL	663	1397	1343	2716	----	1334	3303	1057
New York NY	854	809	1559	2794	1334	----	2841	237
Seattle WA	2625	2052	2131	1134	3303	2841	----	2721
Washington DC	618	709	1307	2646	1057	237	2721	----

Mike: *How long does it take to drive from Atlanta to New York?*
Judy: *It takes about 17 hours.*

Anticipatory It 14

49

1. Mike: _____
   Judy: _____
2. Mike: _____
   Judy: _____
3. Mike: _____
   Judy: _____
4. Mike: _____
   Judy: _____
5. Mike: _____
   Judy: _____

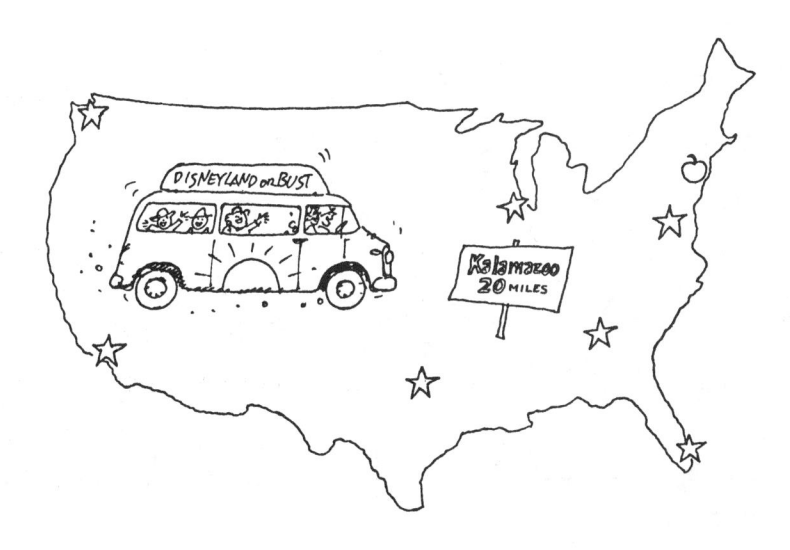

6. Mike: _____
   Judy: _____
7. Mike: _____
   Judy: _____
8. Mike: _____
   Judy: _____

Vocabulary Summary

convenient	(on) foot	infinite	theater
discover	get around	kiosk	tour
dream	get used to	pace (of life)	uncooperative
effort	half-price	packaged	unforgettable
energy	hazardous	perception	wise
event	hospitable	senses	wonders
exciting	hustle and	subway	
fabulous	bustle	tense (adj.)	

15 Future without future tense   50
Extracurricular activities

"Real" time and grammatical tense are not always the same. The **going to** future and the **will** future are grammatical tenses that refer to future time, but future time can also be expressed in these ways:

1. simple present, especially of verbs concerning arrival and departure*

   *What time **does** the team bus **leave** for tonight's game?*

2. present progressive of action verbs*

   *Who's **playing** in the starting lineup?*

3. present of **be + about to**, which expresses the immediate future

   *They're **about to** announce the Most Valuable Player award.*

*The context or the use of specific future time expressions (**tonight, tomorrow, next week,** etc.) will usually indicate whether these refer to future time.

A. Mark with **X** those sentences that clearly refer to future time.

____ 1. After our first morning class, some of us go to the coffee shop.
____ 2. The bus for the ball game goes at 7:30 tonight.
____ 3. When are you leaving for the meeting of the Young Republican Association?
____ 4. The Association of Young Democrats is meeting at eight o'clock Thursday.
____ 5. The Music Appreciation Club meets every other Friday.
____ 6. The chamber music series ends May 28.
____ 7. What are you doing?
____ 8. What are you doing after this evening's lecture?
____ 9. I'm about to sign up for the basketball team.
____ 10. Our soccer team stands second in our division.
____ 11. We're organizing a party for Saturday night.
____ 12. What time does the concert start?
____ 13. Sssh. The concert is beginning.

Future time without future tense 15

___ 14. Come on, everybody's outside playing touch football.

___ 15. The Governor is coming to speak to the Political Science Organization next semester.

B. Rewrite each sentence with the verb in simple present and in present progressive.

The anthropology lecture series will begin Wednesday.
  a. *The anthropology lecture series begins Wednesday.*
  b. *The anthropology lecture series is beginning Wednesday.*

1. Rehearsals for "Joe Egg" are going to start this afternoon at 3:30.
   a. _____
   b. _____

2. Marching band members will leave at 10 for the state competition.
   a. _____
   b. _____

3. Everybody going out for intramural basketball will meet in the gym today at 4.
   a. _____
   b. _____

4. What time is the lecture going to end?
   a. _____
   b. _____

5. The archeology club is going to have three guest lecturers next semester.
   a. _____
   b. _____

15 Future time without future tense 52

C. Rewrite each sentence with **about to.**

I'm so disgusted with my performance that I'm going to quit the debate team!

I'm so disgusted with my performance that I'm about to quit the debate team!

1. The jazz group sounds so bad that I'm going to try out for it myself.

2. Have you ever noticed how many of our guest lecturers clear their throats when they're going to speak?

3. These school romances   Did you know that Harvey is going to break up with Tricia?

4. Poor Berta is so far behind that it looks as though she's going to have to drop out of the marathon.

Vocabulary Summary

association	drop out (of)	meeting	sign up (for)
award	go out (for)	Most Valuable	soccer
basketball	gym	Player	team
break up (with)	intramural	organization	touch football
chamber music	jazz	organize	try out (for)
club	lecture	program	tutoring
competition	lecturer	rehearsal	
concert	lineup	romance	
debate	marathon	semester	
division	marching band	series	

16 Past progressive tense

A waiter's life

> We <u>form</u> the past progressive by using the past of the verb **be** (**was** or **were**) + the present participle (**-ing** form) of the main verb.
>
>   I/He/She/It **was** eat**ing**.
>   We/You/They **were** eat**ing**.
>
> We <u>use</u> the past progressive to indicate that a temporary, continuing past action was happening at the time of another activity in the past or at a specific time in the past.
>
> *We **were** calmly **eating** our dinner at Chez Nous **when** firefighters **burst in** to put out a kitchen fire. (**While** we **were** calmly **eating** our dinner at Chez Nous, firefighters **burst in** to put out a kitchen fire.)**
> *The people at the next tables **were having** after-dinner drinks **as** the firefighters **were bringing** in hoses from their trucks.*
> ***Meanwhile**, the maitre d' **was running around** trying to keep everyone calm.*
>
> *Note the use of **when** and **while** or **as** and the difference between continuing actions ("were eating," "were having" "were bringing in," "was running around") and more sudden, instantaneous action ("burst in").

Write each verb in parentheses in the **appropriate** tense, either simple past or past progressive. In some cases, either is possible.

    I _____(work) as a waiter at the Chez Nous for about five years, and a lot of peculiar things _____ (happen) while I _____(work) there. One time a fire _____ (start) in the kitchen, so we immediately _____ (call) the fire department. When they _____(get) there, Max, the maitre d', _____ (tear around) trying to keep everybody calm, but actually nobody else _____ (be) excited. Even as the firefighters _____ (bring in) hoses, the people at one table _____ (drink) their after-dinner liqueurs, the people at another table _____ placidly _____ (eat) their lamb chops, and a woman and a man at another table _____(be) deep in conversation. I'm not sure that any of them even _____ (notice) what _____ (happen). Suddenly smoke _____ (begin) to billow out into the dining room, but still, none of the customers _____ (move). I

16 Past progressive tense   54

_____ (can't) believe it. I finally _____ (go) to each table and _____ (suggest) that they might like to pay their bills. By the time everybody _____ (get out of) there, the dining room _____ (be) full of smoke. The man and woman _____ still _____ (talk) as they _____ (go) out the door. After all that, they _____ even _____ (not leave) a tip.

   Another time, I had been on duty for a couple of hours. It _____ (be) lunchtime, so the place _____ (be) really crowded. All the time, I _____ (run) back and forth between the kitchen and the dining room and from one table to another. I _____ (see) that some people _____ (look) at me a

55 Past progressive tense 16

little strangely, and some of them _____ even _____ (laugh), but I _____ (be) so busy that I _____ (not pay) attention while all of this _____ (go on). Eventually, one of the customers _____ (call) me over quietly and _____ (whisper), "Waiter, _____ you _____ (dress) in a hurry this morning? I think you should know that your fly is unzipped."

Then there was the time, about two nights after I first _____ (go) to work at Chez Nous, when I _____ (wait on) a table of really important people: the mayor of the city and the attorney general of the state, with their husbands. First, while I _____ (give out) the menus, the mayor's husband _____ (say), "Well, how _____ (be) your day today?" I _____ (not realize) that he _____ (not talk) to me, so I _____ (say), "Pretty good, thanks, and yours?" He _____ (look at) me very coldly and _____ (ask), "_____ I _____ (address) you, young man?" I _____ (apologize) profusely, of course, but I _____ (have to) apologize even more profusely later. I _____ (carry) a big tray with all of their dinners on it when I _____ (trip) over something near their table and _____ (fall) forward. A roast duck _____ (land) in the attorney general's husband's lap, I _____ (knock) a big bowl of soup into the mayor's open purse, which _____ (sit) on the floor next to her, and with my elbow, I _____ (dislodge) the attorney general's wig. There _____ (be) quite an uproar. I guess nobody _____ (know) before that she _____ (be) almost bald.

Vocabulary Summary

apologize	elbow	lamb chop	put out
attorney general	eventually	land (v.)	roast
back and forth	firefighter	lap (of a person)	suddenly
bald	fly (of trousers)	liqueur	tear around
billow	get out of	maitre d'	tip
burst in	give out (hand out)	mayor	trip (stumble)
calmly		meanwhile	unzipped
coldly	go on (happen)	pay attention (to)	uproar
dislodge	hose	peculiar	wait on
duck (fowl)	immediately	placidly	whisper
(on) duty	knock into	profusely	wig

17 Present perfect tense

Tooth troubles

We <u>form</u> the present perfect tense by using **have** or **has** (contractions: 've, 's) + the past participle of the main verb. For regular verbs, the past participle form is the same as the past tense form. See the appendix for the forms of common irregular verbs.

*My dentist **has been** in the same location for thirty years.* (irregular)
*Dr. Black, her brother, **has moved** five times since 1955.* (regular)

We <u>use</u> the present perfect tense when there is some connection in the speaker's or writer's mind between the past and the present, specifically when:

1. an action or state began in the past and continues into the present.

   *I've **had** this toothache since Wednesday.*

2. an action has been repeated in the past.

   *I've already **been** to the dentist six times this year.*

3. an action was completed very recently.

   *I've just **called** for another appointment.*

These time expressions are often used with present perfect. Notice their positions in the sample sentences.

how long

How long has your dentist had her office in that building?

for, since   Use **for** with a duration of time. Use **since** with a definite time in the past.

*My dentist has been in the same location **for thirty years**.*
*She's been there **since she began her practice**.*

so far, up 'til/to now, in (one's) **life**

*Up to now she's been the best dentist I've had **in my life**.*

Present perfect tense 17

already, yet Use **already** in affirmative statements and in questions. Use **yet** in negative statements and in questions.

> *I've **already been** to the dentist six times this year, but my wife **hasn't been** there **yet**.*

lately, recently, just, finally

> *However, her teeth haven't needed work **recently**.*

sometimes, usually, never, ever, etc. Use these frequency adverbs when both past and present are included. Use **ever** in questions and in negative statements.

> *Up 'til now our dentist has **usually** asked to see her only once a year.*

Contrast the present perfect with the simple past tense, which refers to a definite time in the past.

> *Have you ever had a wisdom tooth pulled? (present perfect)*
> *I had one out a couple of years ago. (simple past)*

A. Fill in the blanks with the present perfect forms of the verbs in parentheses.

My dentist _has been_ in the same location for thirty years. (be)

1. She'___ always _____ in the treatment of gum disease. (specialize)
2. I'm sorry I'm running behind schedule. I hope you _____ very long. (not wait)
3. How long _____ it _____ since we' _____ X-rays of your teeth? (be, take)
4. _____ you _____ a checkup lately? (have)
5. I'_____ toothpaste with fluoride since it first came out. (use)
6. I don't think I'_____ ever _____ such a good set of teeth in my life. (see)
7. _____ she _____ rid of her toothache yet? (get)
8. He'_____ already _____ to his dentist five times so far this year. (go)
9. I'_____ always _____ my teeth at least three times a day. (brush)

17 Present perfect tense 58

B. Rewrite these conversations with the time expressions in parentheses. In some cases, you will have to choose between two expressions.

    Cyrus: Have you been to a dentist? (lately)
    Miles: I haven't been last fall. (for/since)
    Cyrus: *Have you been to the dentist lately?*
    Miles: *I haven't been since last fall.*

1. **Dr. Po:** Have you had this problem? (how long)
    Miles: Almost a week. (for/since)
    Dr. Po: _____
    Miles: _____

2. **Dr. Po:** Tell me if this hurts.
    Miles: You haven't hurt me, but I'll let you know. (already/yet)
    Dr. Po: _____
    Miles: _____

3. **Dr. Po:** Have you had root canal work done? (ever)
    Miles: No, I have, and I don't want to. (never)
    Dr. Po: _____
    Miles: _____

4. **Cyrus:** Why is your mouth moving so strangely as you talk?
    Miles: I've come from having a cavity filled, and the dentist gave me novocain. (just)
    Cyrus: _____
    Miles: _____

5. **Dr. Po:** Have you taken such good care of your teeth? (always)
    Cyrus: No. I paid $400 in dentist bills last year. (for/since)
    Dr. Po: _____
    Cyrus: _____

6. **Cyrus:** Haven't you started drilling, Doctor? (already/yet)
    Dr. Po: These new drills are amazing. I've stopped. (already/yet)
    Cyrus: _____
    Dr. Po: _____

7. **Ms. Po:** How many payments have you made on your bill? (up to now)
    Elinor: All of them. I've made my last payment. (finally)
    Ms. Po: _____
    Elinor: _____

Present perfect tense 17

8. **Cyrus:** Have you lost this filling? (recently)
   Elinor: Yes, it dropped out yesterday afternoon. (just)
   Cyrus: _____
   Elinor: _____

9. **Ruth:** How long has it been the hygienist has seen you? (for/since)
   Elinor: I haven't had my teeth cleaned about a year now. (for/since)
   Ruth: _____
   Elinor: _____

10. **Ms. Po:** How many times has your son been to the orthodontist? (so far)
    Ruth: Let's see. He's been there three times. (up 'til now)
    Ms. Po: _____
    Ruth: _____

11. **Noah:** Has your dentist been on time for your appointments? (usually)
    Miles: I don't think he's started on time. (ever; already/yet) He's run late. (every time, so far)
    Noah: _____
    Miles: _____

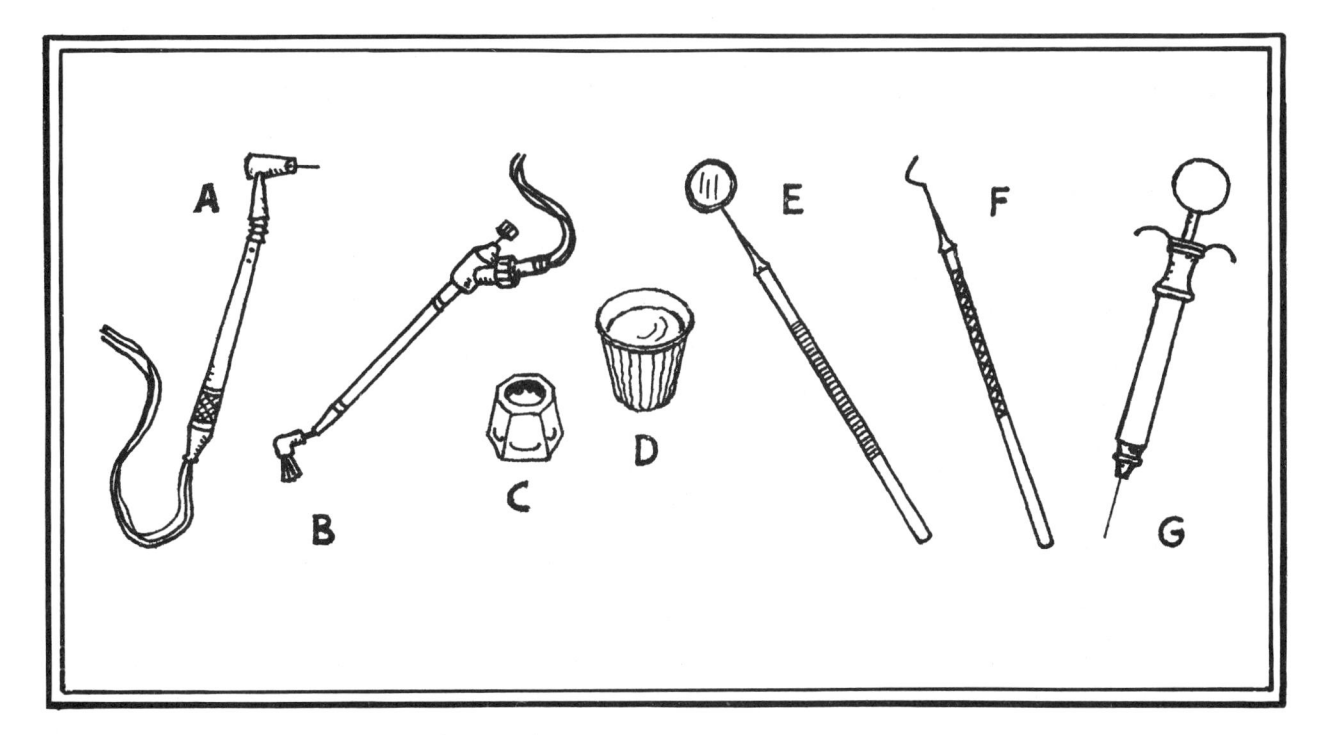

Have you already learned the names of these dentist's tools?
What are they called?

A. _____ B. _____ C. _____
D. _____ E. _____ F. _____
               G. _____

17   Present perfect tense   60

C. Fill in the blanks with the simple past or the present perfect of the verbs in parentheses.

I __went__ the dentist Tuesday. (go)

1. That's the first time I _____ there since August. (be)
2. Some of us _____ the names for teeth when we were in school: canines, incisors, bicuspids, etc. (learn)
3. How long _____ your town _____ fluoridated water? (have)
4. I have to buy some hydrogen peroxide. The hygienist _____ just _____ me to brush with a solution of that and baking soda. (tell)
5. How many times _____ you _____ your dentist so far this year? (see)
6. How many times _____ you _____ him last year? (see)
7. _____ anything about your teeth _____ you lately, or is everything O.K.? (bother)
8. One of my back lower teeth _____ a little sensitive for a few days last week, but that's all. (be)
9. During those few days, _____ it _____ with hot or cold or both? (hurt)
10. _____ you always _____ to floss after every meal? (remember)
11. _____ anyone in your family ever _____ similar problems? (experience)
12. What _____ your dentist _____ you yesterday? (tell)
13. She _____ that my teeth _____ in pretty good condition, but I still need to have a couple of cavities filled. (say, be)

Vocabulary Summary

appointment	filling	novocain	solution
brush	floss	orthodontist	specialize
cavity	fluoridated	payment	take care of
checkup	fluoride	practice	toothache
dentist	get rid of	pull	toothpaste
disease	gum	root canal	treatment
drill	have (a tooth) out	run behind	wisdom tooth
drop out	hurt	run late	X-ray
fill	hygienist	sensitive	

Past perfect tense

Ancient history

The past perfect tense is formed with **had** (contraction: **'d**) + the past participle (See lesson 17) of the main verb.

> *There is evidence that other sailors or explorers **had visited** North America hundreds of years before Columbus.*

It expresses an activity or a state that occurred before another in the past or before a specific time in the past.

> ***By 900 A.D.**, the Mayans **had developed** a high civilization in what is now Guatemala.*

The following time expressions are often used in sentences with the past perfect.

before*

> *The Indus civilization in India **had begun** to decline before Aryan invaders destroyed it.*

after*

> *After Diocletian **had become** emperor, he divided the Byzantine Empire into two parts.*

as soon as*

> *Hannibal invaded Italy as soon as he **had crossed** the Alps.*

when/by the time

> *When/By the time Greek civilization developed, the Olmec civilization **had existed** in Mexico for several hundred years.*

already/yet

> *During the same period, the Chinese **had** already **developed** a writing system, whereas the North Europeans had not yet learned to write.*

just

> *The Sumerians **had** just **learned** to use copper when they also began using bronze.*

*In informal speech, simple past is often used in place of past perfect.

18 Past perfect tense

A. In each sentence, use simple past in one blank and past perfect in the other.

Before Caesar __defeated__ Pompey in 48 B.C., they __had fought__ for control of Rome. (defeat, fight)

1. Caesar _____ dictator of Rome when conspirators led by Brutus and Cassius _____ him. (become, kill)
2. When it _____ finally complete, about 600 A.D., work on the Talmud ____ 500 years. (be, take)
3. Mycenae and other cities in Greece and Asia Minor _____ elements of Minoan culture, which _____ 1,400 years before. (keep, emerge)
4. When Nubia _____, it _____ an independent kingdom for 1,000 years. (fall, be)
5. Alexander the Great _____ most of the known world by the time he _____ 33 years old. (already conquer, be)
6. During the Hellenistic period, scientific knowledge _____ rapidly, especially at Alexandria, where the Ptolemies _____ a great library and museum. (grow, build)
7. When Rome _____ its victory over Egypt in the first century B.C., it _____ control of Greece and Asia Minor in the 2nd century B.C. (win, already get)

Can you name these leaders of the ancient world?

A. _____ B. _____ C. _____

D. _____ E. _____

Past perfect tense 18

8. Soon after Mohammed _____ his hegira to Median, he _____ the first jihad, a holy war, in 624 A.D. (make, declare)

9. At the time Constantine II _____ as Roman Emperor, his father, Constantine the Great, _____ Christianity as the religion of the Empire. (take over, establish)

10. By the time the second millennium B.C. _____ to an end, the earliest Arab culture _____ in Yemen. (come, appear)

11. Centuries before the Renaissance _____ in Europe, a brilliant, cosmopolitan Arab Moslem civilization _____ in Baghdad. (begin, begin)

12. The Yamato clan _____ the Japanese states after Chinese or Koreans _____ the Yayoi period. (unite, introduce)

13. The Axum kingdom in Ethiopia _____ the Red Sea coast before Egypt _____ Axum's political and economic ties with Byzantium. (control, cut)

14. Charlemagne _____ interest in commerce and the arts, which _____ into decline. (reawaken, go)

15. Europe _____ an end of the Dark Ages when extremely advanced civilizations _____ on other continents. (not/yet/see, flourish)

Vocabulary Summary

A.D.	control	fall	Minoan
ancient	culture	fight	Moslem
Arab	decline	flourish	Mycenae
Aryan	defeat	Greek	Nubia
Asia Minor	destroy	Hellenistic	Olmec
Axum	develop	history	period
B.C.	dictator	Indus	Ptolemies
Byzantine	Egypt	introduce	Rome
century	emerge	invade	Sumerian
Chinese	emperor	invader	system
Christianity	empire	Japanese	take over
civilization	establish	kingdom	Talmud
clan	evidence	Korean	unite
conquer	exist	Mayan	
conquest	explorer	millenium	

19 Future perfect; perfect progressive

Class reunion

1. We <u>form</u> the future perfect with **will have** + the past participle of the main verb (see lesson 17).

    *In June, our class **will have been** out of high school for ten years.*

   We <u>use</u> the future perfect to express a future time that comes before another future time. It generally represents a continuation of an action that began in the past. Time expressions with prepositions such as **at, by,** and **before** usually accompany the future perfect. They indicate when the action will be completed.

    *Our tenth reunion committee has been meeting monthly. By the time of the reunion, it **will have met** six times.*

2. We <u>form</u> the perfect progressive tenses like this:

    present perfect progressive: **have/has been** + the **-ing** form of the main verb

    past perfect progressive: **had been** + the **-ing** form of the main verb

    future perfect progressive: **will have been** + the **-ing** form of the main verb

   We <u>use</u> the perfect progressive tenses to emphasize the continuous nature of an activity.

    *The committee **has been meeting** at Jeanette Chandler's house.*
    *It **had been meeting** at Will Davis's house until he got sick.*
    *By the time of the reunion, the committee **will have been working** for six months.*

19 Future perfect; perfect progressive forms

A. These are some of the things the class reunion committee had to do:

1. Meet monthly.
2. Invite former faculty.
3. Track down all alumnae and alumni.
4. Send out notices to everyone.
5. Hire a band.
6. Reserve the restaurant.
7. Work out the menu.
8. Get a skit ready.
9. Make name tags.
10. Buy prizes.

Write ten sentences about what members of the committee will have done by the time of their reunion. Use the above list.

1. _____
2. _____
3. _____
4. _____
5. _____
6. _____
7. _____
8. _____
9. _____
10. _____

B. These are parts of conversations heard at the class reunion. Rewrite them, using perfect progressive forms of the verbs in parentheses.

Rose: How long _____ you _____ in Boston? (live)
Rick: For almost two years now.
Rose: *How long have you been living in Boston?*
Rick: *For almost two years now.*

1. **Rose:** Did you tell me where you _____ before that? I don't remember. (live)
   Rick: In Salt Lake City.
   Rose: _____
   Rick: _____

2. **Rose:** _____ you _____ for Acme very long? (work)
   Rick: Let's see, in September I _____ for them for six years. (work)

19 Future perfect; perfect progressive forms 66

Rose: _____

Rick: _____

3. **Rose:** I remember that at the last reunion, you _____ very well for a while. (not feel)

   Rick: That's right, but lately, I _____ fine. (feel)

   Rose: _____

   Rick: _____

4. **Rose:** _____ you and your wife _____ better than you were last year? (get along)

   Rick: I'm afraid not. We _____ getting divorced. (talk about)

   Rose: _____

   Rick: _____

5. **Sam:** So you'll be getting your college degree next year?

   Mick: Finally. At that point, I _____ it for seven years, off and on. (work toward)

   Sam: _____

   Mick: _____

6. **Fran:** Look at Dorothea! What _____ her? (happen to)

   Tammy: She told me on the phone that she _____ a lot of weight. Now I can believe it. (put on)

   Fran: _____
   _____

   Tammy: _____

7. **Fran:** You look different. Did you always wear glasses?

   Tammy: This fall, I _____ them for twenty-five years. (wear)

   Fran: _____

   Tammy: _____

8. **Fran:** When are you expecting your baby?

   Tammy: In two months. At last. You know, we _____ to have children for years, and we'd just about given up. (try)

   Fran: _____

   Tammy: _____
   _____

9. **Tom:** _____ you _____ much golf lately? (play)

   Saul: I _____ much at all for a while, but then I started up again this spring. (not play)

   Tom: _____

   Saul: _____
   _____

67 Future perfect; perfect progressive forms 19

10. **Fran:** I see that Cornell is here alone again. _____ he _____ _____ somebody? (not go out with)

    Tammy: He _____ Lucille, but they _____ each other for a few months now. (go out with, not see)

    Fran: _____

    Tammy: _____

11. **Rick:** _____ you _____ that the women in our class _____ better than the men? The women look terrific. (notice, hold up)

    Sky: You're right. It looks as if all the women _____ weight, and all the men _____ their hair. (lose, lose)

    Rick: _____

    Sky: _____

Vocabulary Summary

alumnae	get divorced	name tag	send out
alumni	give up	notice	skit
band	go out with	(be) out of (no	start up
class	hire	longer in)	track down
committee	hold up (maintain	prize	wear glasses
degree	oneself)	put on weight	work toward
expect a baby	lose one's hair	reserve	
faculty	lose weight	see (have dates	
get along	monthly	with)	

20 Customary past and present   68
Changing times

> **Used to** + the simple form of the verb expresses an activity or a state of the past that no longer occurs.
>
> *Before TV, families **used to spend** time doing things together, but they don't seem to anymore.*
>
> Use the auxiliary **do** with questions and negative statements.
>
> ***Did** you **use to have** an imaginary friend when you were little?*
> *No, I **didn't**. **Did** you?*
>
> **Would** (contraction: **'d**) + the simple form of the verb expresses a habit or custom of the past.
>
> *My imaginary friend was called Florinda. **I'd talk** to her as if she were real.*
>
> Forms of **be** + **used to** + noun, pronoun, or gerund (the noun **-ing** form of the verb) express habits or customs that may be of the past or the present, depending on the tense of **be**.
>
> ***Are** you **used to staying up** late?*
> *I **was** when I was younger, but **I'm** not **used to it** anymore.*

A. Rewrite the conversation with **used to** for each underlined verb.

Tim: What are some things you <u>did</u> when you were a little boy, Grandpa? What kind of games did you <u>play</u>?

Grandpa: Oh, let's see. There <u>was</u> a gang of boys in my neighborhood. We <u>played</u> a lot of baseball and touch football, of course. My family <u>spent</u> time together, too, playing games. We <u>had</u> all kinds of card games. Not regular playing cards, because my parents didn't <u>allow</u> those, but games like Flinch and Rook and Authors.

Tim: Didn't you <u>watch</u> TV?

Grandpa: This was the Dark Ages, Tim. There <u>wasn't</u> any TV then. Believe it or not, we <u>listened</u> to the radio, especially Sunday nights.

<u>What are some of the things you used to do when you were a</u>

Customary past and present 20

little boy, Grandpa?

B. Rewrite the paragraph with **would** for each underlined verb. Use the contraction.

Tim: What are some of your happiest memories from when you were young, Grandma?

Grandma: The first thing I think of is times I spent with my younger brother. During the summer, we often <u>went</u> out to Vanderling Lake together, just the two of us. We <u>carried</u> a picnic lunch and we <u>swam</u> and <u>hiked</u> for a while, and then we <u>ate</u> our lunch. Once in a while we <u>took</u> our bikes as we got a little older. I <u>fixed</u> a couple of sandwiches, and we <u>put</u> them in the basket on my bike, and we <u>stopped</u> at the drugstore and <u>got</u> big milkshakes in cartons. We <u>went</u> out to the lake and <u>sat</u> there and <u>watched</u> the lake and <u>ate</u> our lunch. It doesn't sound like much now, but we always <u>had</u> a good time.

20 Customary past and present

C. Paul filled out a questionnaire about his daily habits like this.

DO YOU USUALLY...	YES	NO
1. ...BEGIN YOUR DAY IN A GOOD MOOD?	☐	☐
2. ...TAKE A SHOWER IN THE MORNING?	☐	☐
3. ...EAT A GOOD, BALANCED BREAKFAST?	☐	☐
4. ...DRINK MORE THAN TWO CUPS OF COFFEE A DAY?	☐	☐
5. ...DRIVE TO WORK?	☐	☐
6. ...WORK ALL MORNING WITHOUT A BREAK?	☐	☐
7. ...CARRY YOUR LUNCH TO WORK?	☐	☐
8. ...FINISH WORK BY 4:30?	☐	☐
9. ...GET HOME TIRED?	☐	☐
10. ...GO OUT IN THE EVENING?	☐	☐

Now write a sentence with **is** or **isn't used to** for each item on the questionnaire.

1. *Paul isn't used to beginning his day in a good mood.*
2.
3.
4.
5.
6.
7.
8.
9.
10.

Customary past and present 20

D. This is information about Paulette's customs and habits. Some were only in the past, others continue into the present, and others are only in the present.

PAST	PRESENT?
1. DIDN'T WRITE A LOT OF LETTERS	YES
2. READ THE NEWSPAPER EVERY DAY	NO
3. WENT TO SCARY MOVIES	YES
4. WASN'T AFRAID OF FLYING	YES
5. RAN AT LEAST TWO MILES A DAY	YES
6. SLEPT EIGHT HOURS A NIGHT	NO
7. DIDN'T PAY BILLS ON TIME	YES
8. SWAM REGULARLY	NO
9. SPOKE IN PUBLIC	YES
10. DIDN'T STUDY ANCIENT HISTORY	YES
11. ATE TOO MUCH	NO
12. FELT AMBITIOUS MOST OF THE TIME	YES

Now write sentences about Paulette's activities.

1. Paulette didn't use to write a lot of letters, but now she does.
2. She used to read the newspapers every day, but she doesn't anymore.
3. She's used to going to scary movies.
4. _____
5. _____
6. _____
7. _____
8. _____
9. _____
10. _____
11. _____
12. _____

21 Past of GOING TO, ABOUT TO

Accident and injuries

> The past of **going to** is formed with **was** or **were**. It describes an intended or planned action that was delayed or never happened.
>
> *Agatha and Melvin **were going to** (were intending/planning to) drive to Omaha today, but they totalled their car yesterday.*
>
> In the negative, it usually describes an action that was not planned but did happen or is going to happen.
>
> *Melvin **wasn't going to** spend the next few days in the hospital, but now he has to.*
>
> It is also used in indirect speech.
>
> *The doctor told Melvin, "You'll be out soon."*
> *The doctor told Melvin that he **was going to** be out soon.*
>
> The past of **about to** is also formed with **was** or **were** and describes an intended action that did not happen. It is often used with **just** because the time between the intention and the "not happening" was very short.
>
> *Clementa **was just about to** climb the last step of the stepladder when she fell and broke her hip.*

A. What does each sentence imply? circle **a** or **b**.

Agatha and Melvin were going to drive to Omaha today.
    a. They did.   (b.) They didn't.

1. Dr. Pangloss was going to play golf this afternoon.
    a. He did.   b. He didn't.

2. He wasn't going to perform emergency surgery on Melvin.
    a. He did.   b. He didn't.

3. Agatha was going to visit the stockyards in Omaha.
    a. She did.   b. She didn't.

4. She wasn't going to visit Melvin in the hospital.
    a. She did.   b. She didn't.

5. Clementa was about to reach the last step of the stepladder.
    a. She did.   b. She didn't.

73 Past of GOING TO, ABOUT TO   21

6. She was about to wash the upper windows.
   a. She did.   b. She didn't.

7. She wasn't going to spend the next eight weeks with her hip in a cast.
   a. She's going to.   b. She isn't going to.

B. Fill in each blank with **going to** or **about to**.

Phil was just _about to_ board the train when he slipped and sprained his ankle.

1. I was _____ make a left turn at the light when it turned red, and I couldn't stop in time.

2. Frannie and Maurice were _____ go on vacation this week, until Frannie stumbled over the dog and broke her arm.

3. Carla wasn't _____ see a doctor about her bruised back, but finally it began to hurt too much.

4. She wasn't _____ take any sedatives or painkillers until the doctor insisted.

5. Kelly was _____ treat the cut on his thigh with just mercurochrome and a bandage, but it turned out to need thirty stitches.

6. Just as Valera was _____ dive into the water, she felt a bone snap in her left knee.

7. I got to my doctor just in time. Infection was _____ set in where my cat had scratched me.

C. Rewrite each sentence with **was/wasn't/were/weren't going to**.

Beryl looked as though she would choke, so Tom applied the Heimlich maneuver.

Beryl looked as though she was going to choke, so Tom applied the Heimlich maneuver.

1. Benjamin and Colleen had started to move the accident victims when Wilhelm warned them not to.

   _____
   _____

2. Lu Ann had intended to study first aid, but she didn't think she had time.

   _____
   _____

21 Past of GOING TO, ABOUT TO 74

3. At first Sybil and Sam hadn't planned to learn CPR, but now they're glad they changed their minds.
   _____
   _____

4. Delmar was afraid he wouldn't survive when he realized he was drowning.
   _____
   _____

5. Foolishly, we started to pick up a snake in the garden without knowing whether it was poisonous.
   _____
   _____

6. Daisy promised her mother that she'd never take barbiturates again.
   _____
   _____

7. It was a relief to hear that the burn victims wouldn't die.
   _____

8. The inexperienced paramedic didn't plan to treat Cora for shock until he remembered that that should be his first priority.
   _____
   _____

9. When I felt heart attack symptoms, I intended to call my own doctor, but I called the volunteer ambulance squad instead because I thought they could get here faster.
   _____
   _____

Vocabulary Summary

accident	CPR (cardio-	infection	snap
ankle	pulmonary	injury	sprain
apply	resuscitation)	knee	squad
arm	cut	mercurochrome	stitch
attack	die	(be) out (of the	stumble (over)
back	drown	hospital)	surgery
bandage	emergency	painkiller	survive
barbiturate	fall	paramedic	symptom
bone	first aid	poisonous	thigh
break	heart	scratch	total (a car)
bruised	Heimlich	sedative	victim
burn	maneuver	shock	volunteer
cast	hip	slip	
choke	hospital	snake	

Modals of obligation/necessity 22

At a hospital

1. **Have to** and **must** express obligation so strong that it is almost a necessity.

   *We **have to** get the family's permission to operate on this woman.*
   *She **must** have an operation at once.*

   Note: **Must** is more formal and stronger than **have to**. In very informal speech, people often use **have got to** in present affirmative sentences:

   *We've **got to** get the family's permission to operate.*

2. **Had to** is the **past affirmative** for both **have to** and **must**.

   *We **had to** get the family's permission to operate.*
   *She **had to** have an operation at once.*

3. The **present negative** of **must** expresses strong prohibition.

   *We **mustn't** delay the operation any longer.*

   The **present negative** of **have to** expresses lack of obligation.

   *You **don't have to** call Dr. Thomas. She's already in the O.R.**

   When a second person is addressed, imperative forms are often used instead of **must**.

   *You **must begin** the operation immediately. / **Begin** the operation immediately.*
   *You **mustn't delay**. / **Don't delay**.*

   *See the vocabulary list for the meanings of abbreviations used in this lesson.

A. Change the doctor's commands to a patient into sentences with **you must** or **you mustn't**.

Stay in bed for at least a week.
You must stay in bed at least a week.

1. Don't exert yourself in any way.

_____

22 Modals of obligation and necessity 76

2. Take these pills after each meal.
   _____

3. Don't have any visitors until Tuesday.
   _____

4. Don't go back to your old habits when you go home.
   _____

5. Take better care of yourself in the future.
   _____

6. Quit smoking.
   _____

7. Get more exercise.
   _____

B. Rewrite the sentences with **have to** and **have got to**.

   Must I have a visitor's card to see a patient here?
   a. *Do I have to have a visitor's card to see a patient here?*
   b. *Have I got to have a visitor's card to see a patient here?*

1. I must see my father right away.
   a. _____
   b. _____

2. He must have surgery in a few hours.
   a. _____
   b. _____

3. My brother and I must talk with him before then.
   a. _____
   b. _____

4. Must we get his doctor's permission?
   a. _____
   b. _____

5. We must find out what the prognosis is.
   a. _____
   b. _____

C. Rewrite each sentence in the past.

   Do you have to have your appendix out?
   Did you have to have your appendix out?

Modals of obligation and necessity 22

1. Yes, but I must stay in the hospital for only three days afterward.
   _____

2. Does Mrs. Brewer have to go to the I.C.U.?
   _____

3. Yes, she has to have care around the clock.
   _____

4. Someone must monitor her vital signs at all times.
   _____

5. Somebody must call an ambulance.
   _____

6. We have to get Mr. Pangborn to the hospital.
   _____

7. He must go to the E.R.
   _____

D. These signs are often seen around hospitals. Complete the sentences below, using **mustn't** or **have to.**

1. You _____ turn right.
2. We _____ watch out for handicapped people.
3. You _____ smoke here.
4. It's one way. We _____ go in the direction of the arrow.
5. You _____ go right to get to the X-ray room.
6. You _____ park here.
7. There are pedestrians. We _____ be careful.
8. To get to the emergency room, you _____ turn right.
9. It's a right turn only. You _____ turn left.
10. There is no U-turn. You _____ try to turn around here.

22 Modals of obligation and necessity

E. This is a conversation between a patient and a doctor. Fill in each blank with a present form of **have to** or **must**, affirmative or negative.

Mrs. Duffy: Can I ask you some questions, Doctor?

Dr. Wilcox: Yes, of course. You _____ ask me about anything that concerns you.

Mrs. Duffy: _____ I _____ have an operation?

Dr. Wilcox: Well, we might _____ do a little exploratory surgery. Then we'll find out whether we _____ operate. My feeling is that we _____ do anything major. You _____ worry, though; that would just make you feel worse.

Mrs. Duffy: If I _____ have the operation, what _____ I _____ do?

Dr. Wilcox: We usually put people with your problem on a mild tranquilizer. Then there are certain foods they _____ eat, especially anything hot or spicy. They should also cut down on carbohydrates, although they _____ avoid them entirely. And they _____ smoke, or drink anything alcoholic or carbonated.

Mrs. Duffy: Are you sure I'll be all right?

Dr. Wilcox: Certainly. You _____ trust me.

Mrs. Duffy: All right, Doctor. I'm in your hands.

Vocabulary Summary

ambulance	exert	medication	pill
appendix	exploratory	mild	prognosis
carbohydrate	habit	monitor	quit
care (n.)	have (something) out	operate	surgery
control	hospital	operation	take care of
cut down on	I.C.U. (Intensive Care Unit)	O.R. (Operating Room)	tranquilizer
diet	major	patient	visitor's card
E.R. (Emergency Room)		permission	vital signs

Modals of advisability/obligation 23
Household chores

1. **Should, ought to**, and **had better** express advisability so strong that it is almost an obligation.

   *I really **should/ought to** mop the floors today, even though I don't feel like it.*

   Had better is less formal and stronger than **should** and **ought to**.

   *I'**d better** fix that step before somebody falls and gets hurt.*

2. The negative forms are **shouldn't, ought not/ought not to**, and **had better not/hadn't better.**

   *I **shouldn't** be sitting here relaxing.*
   *I **ought not (to)** be sitting here relaxing.*
   *I'**d better not/hadn't better** put off fixing the step.*

3. Only **should** is generally used in questions of advisability or obligation.

   ***Should** I wax the floors too? Do you think they need it?*

4. When **shouldn't** and **hadn't better** are used in questions with **you**, they are suggestions.

   ***Shouldn't you/Hadn't you better** sweep the floors before you mop them?*

Vocabulary Summary

basement	furniture	put up	throw away
bathroom	kitchen	rake	tool
clean	lawn	scouring powder	trash
dining room	mop	step	tub
dust	oil	storm window	vacuum
fix	paint	straighten up	wax
floor	put off	sweep	weed

23 Modals of advisability and obligation

A. This is Chris and Walter's list of household chores to be done this weekend.

> **Things To Do!**
>
> <u>Inside</u>
> 1. Dust furniture
> 2. Sweep, mop, and wax kitchen and bathroom floors
> 3. Vacuum other floors
> 4. Clean bathroom
> 5. Straighten up basement
>
> <u>Outside</u>
> 6. Rake leaves
> 7. Mow lawn
> 8. Fix and paint back steps
> 9. Weed vegetable garden
> 10. Put up storm windows

Write sentences with **should** for the inside jobs. Add necessary articles.
1. They should dust the furniture.
2. _____
3. _____
4. _____
5. _____

Write sentences with **ought to** for the outside jobs. Add necessary articles.
6. _____
7. _____
8. _____
9. _____
10. _____

Modals of advisability and obligation 23

B. Imagine that you're Chris or Walter. It's now 2 p.m. Saturday. You've finished some of the chores: 2, 3, 6, and 7. You're already exhausted, but you want to finish the list so you can relax tomorrow. Write sentences about what you'd still better do.

We'd still better dust the furniture.

1. _____
2. _____
3. _____
4. _____
5. _____

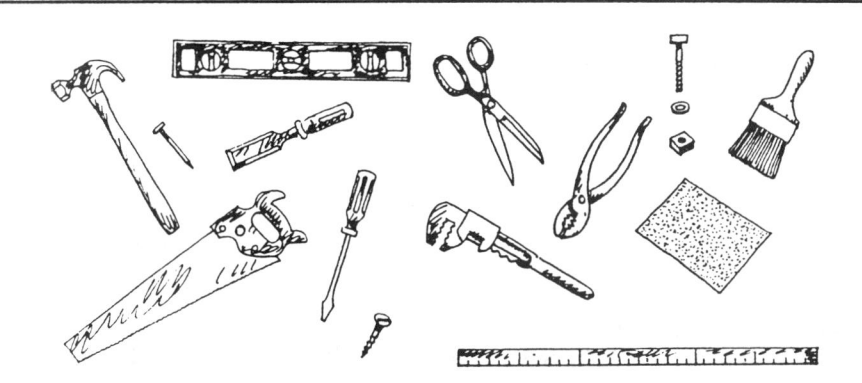

C. As they work, Chris and Walter give each other instructions and warnings. Change them to sentences with **should** and **shouldn't**.

Don't try to carry all those leaves by yourself.
You shouldn't try to carry all those leaves by yourself.

1. Don't walk on the kitchen floor while it's still wet.
   _____

2. Vacuum before you dust.
   _____

3. Throw away some of those old tools that you don't use anymore.
   _____

4. Don't use scouring powder on the tub.
   _____

D. Now change your answers in exercise C to sentences with **had better** or **had better not.**

You'd better not try to carry all those leaves by yourself.

1. _____
2. _____
3. _____
4. _____

23 Modals of advisability and obligation

E. Chris and Walter also ask each other for advice. Change each sentence to a question with **should**.

I don't know whether to try to fix this old lamp or throw it away.
Should I try to fix this old lamp or throw it away.

1. I don't know whether to burn the leaves or put them out with the trash.

2. I can't decide whether to paint the steps gray or black.

3. I'm not sure whether to use wax or oil on the dining room table.

4. I wonder whether to put up the rest of the storm windows now or wait until Monday.

F. Imagine again that you're Chris or Walter. Respond to the questions above in exercise E by making suggestions with **shouldn't** and **hadn't better**. Base your suggestion on the information given.

The old lamp isn't worth fixing.
a. *Shouldn't you throw it away?*
b. *Hadn't you better throw it away?*

1. It's against the law to burn leaves.
   a.
   b.

2. Black will show the dirt more than gray will.
   a.
   b.

3. Oil is better than wax for furniture.
   a.
   b.

4. The weather forecast is for rain on Monday.
   a.
   b.

Modals of preference 24

83

Washington, D.C.

> **Would rather** expresses preference and is followed by the simple form of the main verb. The negative form is **would rather not**.
>
> *Would you rather drive or take the train to Washington?*
> *I'd rather take the train. I'd rather not drive.*
>
> **Would like** politely expresses desire and is followed by an infinitive (phrase) or a noun (phrase).
>
> *I'd like to have lunch at one of the outdoor cafes.*
> *I'd like lunch at one of the outdoor cafes.*
>
> **Would like** in yes/no questions with **you** expresses an invitation.
>
> *Would you like to go to the Smithsonian after lunch?*

A. Using the information in parentheses, write questions and answers with **would rather**. Answer with two sentences, one with **would rather** and the other with **would rather not**.

(go to the Lincoln Memorial -- Jefferson Memorial first)
Aaron: *Would you rather go to the Lincoln Memorial or the Jefferson Memorial first?*
Hal: *I'd rather go to the Jefferson Memorial first. I'd rather not go to the Lincoln Memorial.*

1. (walk -- take a cab)
   Seth: _____
   Roger: _____

2. (visit the National Gallery tomorrow -- the National Air and Space Museum)
   Jeff: _____
   Ginger: _____

3. (climb the stairs to the top of the Washington Monument -- take the elevator)
   Mel: _____
   Enos: _____

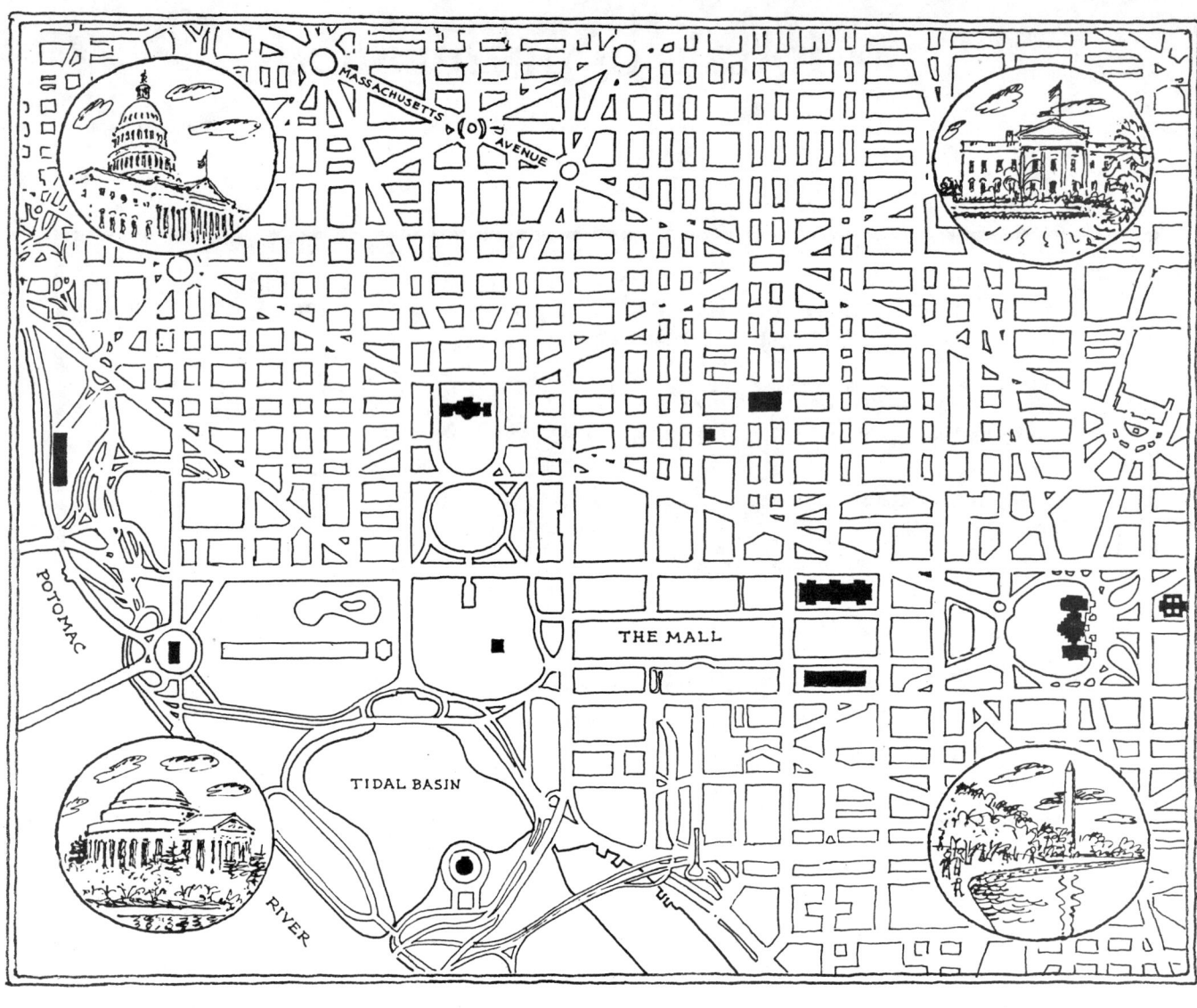

4. (tour the White House -- the Capitol Building)

   Irene: _____

   Kellie: _____

   _____

5. (use a tour bus while we're here -- find our own way around)

   Lance: _____

   Laurel: _____

   _____

6. (have lunch in a restaurant -- have a picnic on the Mall)

   Ginger: _____

   Seth: _____

   _____

7. (go to Georgetown for a side trip -- Arlington National Cemetery)

   Kim: _____

   Hal: _____

   _____

Modals of preference 24

B. Express a desire to do each of the following:

see Ford's Theater, where Lincoln was shot
I'd like to see Ford's Theater, where Lincoln was shot.

1. visit the graves of John and Robert Kennedy

2. look at the paintings at the National Portrait Gallery

3. go to a concert at Kennedy Center

4. see the embassies along Massachusetts Avenue

5. watch a session of Congress

C. Invite someone to do each of the following:

see the cherry blossoms around the Tidal Basin
Would you like to see the cherry blossoms around the Tidal Basin?

1. visit the Supreme Court

2. look at the models at the Patent Building

3. hear one of the military bands play

4. listen to people broadcasting on the Voice of America

5. rest for a while after all this sightseeing

Vocabulary Summary

band (musical)	Congress	model (miniature)	session
broadcast	elevator	monument	side trip
cab	embassy	museum	sightseeing
cafe	gallery	national	Supreme Court
Capitol	grave (n.)	outdoor	theater
cemetery	Mall	painting	tour bus
cherry blossom	memorial	patent	White House
concert	military	portrait	

25 Modals of possibility

Picking out a gift

86

---

1. **Can** usually expresses possibility when the subject is not a person. **Could, may,** and **might** express possibility more generally.

    A: *What should I get Harriet for her birthday?*
    B: *Why not just give her a check? Money **can** be very welcome.*
    A: *I don't know. Harriet **might** be insulted. She **may** not speak to me again if I don't pick out something special.*
    B: *You **could** be right.*

2. All negative forms express negative possibility. The negative contracted forms of **can** and **could** are **can't** (**cannot**) and **couldn't**. The negative forms of **may** and **might** are **may not** and **might not**. **May not** is never contracted. **Might not** (**mightn't**) is usually not contracted.

3. **May**, as a modal of possibility, does not occur in questions.

A. Rewrite each sentence, first with **can** (**can't**), then with **could** (**couldn't**).

It's possible for a fur coat to be a welcome gift.
  a. *A fur coat can be a welcome gift.*
  b. *A fur coat could be a welcome gift.*

1. Sure, and it's possible for it to be prohibitively expensive, too.
   a. _____
   b. _____

2. It's possible for a negligee to be acceptable.
   a. _____
   b. _____

3. I think it's possible for it to be too personal.
   a. _____
   b. _____

4. It isn't possible for that to be the purse I bought you ten years ago. It looks new!
   a. _____
   b. _____

Modals of possibility 25

5. Oh, yes, it's possible.
   a. _____
   b. _____

6. It isn't possible for it to be our anniversary already!
   a. _____
   b. _____

B. Rewrite each sentence in four ways: with **may**, with **may not**, with **might**, and with **might not**.

Maybe Giselle will like the perfume I got her.
   a. *Giselle may like the perfume I got her.*
   b. *Giselle may not like the perfume I got her.*
   c. *Giselle might like the perfume I got her.*
   d. *Giselle might not like the perfume I got her.*

1. Maybe this gold chain will be the perfect present for my nephew.
   a. _____
   b. _____
   c. _____
   d. _____

2. Maybe Mom will want flowers for Mother's Day again this year.
   a. _____
   b. _____
   c. _____
   d. _____

25 Modals of possibility

3. Maybe Horatio will appreciate getting a gift certificate.
   a. _____
   b. _____
   c. _____
   d. _____

4. Maybe this shirt will fit Marcus.
   a. _____
   b. _____
   c. _____
   d. _____

5. Maybe I'm getting a car from my relatives for graduation.
   a. _____
   b. _____
   c. _____
   d. _____

Vocabulary Summary

acceptable	expensive	Mother's Day	present
anniversary	fur coat	negligee	prohibitively
birthday	gift	perfume	purse
chain	gift certificate	personal	welcome
check	gold	pick out	

Modals of probability/inference 26
Drawing conclusions

> 1. **Should** and **ought to** for probability are generally used with **be**, in affirmative statements. They can express present or future probability.
>
> *I hope nothing's happened to the Corleones. They were supposed to be here for dinner at 7:30. It's now 7:45. They **should/ought to** be here by now. Certainly they **ought to/should** be getting here very shortly—unless they've met with some misfortune.*
>
> 2. **Must** for probability or inference expresses greater certainty than **should** or **ought to**. It is used only for affirmative or negative present statements of inference. The negative is not contracted: **must not**.
>
> *You know, I don't remember that Mr. Corleone has ever had a job. He **must** have an independent source of income. He **must not** have to work.*

A. Write **advisability** or **probability** for each use of **should** or **ought to**.

_____ 1. You shouldn't draw conclusions without evidence.

_____ 2. I ought to be fixing the back steps now, not relaxing.

_____ 3. The car keys ought to be on the dresser where I left them.

_____ 4. Should we let the kids stay up late tonight for a change?

_____ 5. The doctor says that Samantha should be feeling better soon.

_____ 6. You shouldn't try to carry that by yourself.

_____ 7. The bakery ought to be on the left-hand side in the next block, if I remember correctly.

_____ 8. We should put your mother's picture out where she can see it when she comes.

_____ 9. Gail should be arriving in Rangoon about now, if her flight is on time.

_____ 10. You ought to enjoy dinner tonight. I made all of your favorite dishes.

26 Modals of probability and inference   90

B. Write **obligation** or **inference** for each use of **must**.

_____ 1. This must be the place Donna and Rick told us about.

_____ 2. I keep forgetting to call Helene. I must do it tonight.

_____ 3. I can't find my wallet. It must be in my other pants.

_____ 4. You must listen when I'm speaking to you.

_____ 5. You must like ice cream. I've never seen a half gallon disappear so fast.

_____ 6. We mustn't blame others for our own mistakes in judgment.

_____ 7. You must look like your father. You don't resemble your mother at all.

_____ 8. All of us must cooperate if this project is going to be a success.

_____ 9. How could I say that? I must not be thinking clearly.

_____ 10. Teachers must consider students' needs when planning lessons.

C. For each item, change the last sentence to a statement of probability or inference with **should**.

Trent's train is due here at 1:58. It's now 1:56. Trent will probably be getting here any minute now.
Trent should be getting here any minute now.

1. I usually leave my house key on the hall table when I come in. It's probably there now.

2. Alastair just went out. He said he was going to return shortly. He'll probably come back within a few minutes.

3. Keiko has been looking for her glasses for fifteen minutes. She'll probably find them soon.

4. The sky is beginning to cloud over, and the temperature is dropping fast. It will probably be snowing before long.

5. My mother gave me $5. That's probably enough for a movie.

91 Modals of probability and inference **26**

Where's the fish?

D. For each item, change the last sentence to a statement of probability or inference with **must**.

I'm sure I was wearing gloves when I came in. I conclude that they're here somewhere.
They must be here somewhere.

1. Bill Grabinsky seems to travel a good deal. I conclude that he has a lot of free time.

2. The Ferlinghettis have tickets for three concert series. I conclude that they enjoy music.

3. Mr. Vandemark looks at me very skeptically when I tell him about the fish I've caught. I conclude that he doesn't believe my stories.

4. I see that Gladys' light is still on. I conclude that she's studying late again.

5. Elizabeth and Phillip used to be good friends, but I noticed that they ignored each other at the meeting yesterday. I conclude that they're not speaking to each other now.

27 Modal of obligation/expectation

The medicine cabinet

Be supposed to + the simple form of the verb expresses:

1. obligation

    *I'm **supposed to take*** *one of these pills every three hours.*

2. expectation

    *The pills **are supposed to work** fast and **relieve** pain quickly.*

This use of the modal sometimes means "be scheduled to":

*My new prescription **is supposed to be** ready at two o'clock.*

In the negative, **be supposed to** expresses:

1. prohibition

    *I'**m not supposed to drive** after taking these pills.*

2. negative expectation

    *The pills **aren't supposed to have** any dangerous side effects.*
    *My new prescription **isn't supposed to be** ready until two o'clock.*

In many cases, **supposed** can be deleted. The meaning is the same.

*I'**m to take** one of these pills every three hours. I'**m not to drive** after taking them.*
*My new prescription **is to be** ready at two o'clock. It **isn't to be** ready until then.*

A. Read the instructions from labels on items in a medicine cabinet. Change each to a statement of obligation or prohibition with the impersonal **you** + **are(n't) supposed to.** Then write the statement again without **supposed.**

Use Fluorex just before bedtime.

    a. _You're supposed to use Fluorex just before bedtime._
    b. _You're to use Fluorex just before bedtime._

1. Brush all tooth surfaces.

    a. _____
    b. _____

27 Modal of obligation and expectation

2. Do not rinse out your mouth after using Fluorex.
   a. _____
   b. _____
3. Do not eat or drink for 30 minutes after use.
   a. _____
   b. _____
4. Repeat this procedure daily.
   a. _____
   b. _____
5. Take 2 tablets every 4 hours.
   a. _____
   b. _____
6. Do not exceed 12 tablets in 24 hours.
   a. _____
   b. _____
7. Drink a full glass of water with each dose.
   a. _____
   b. _____
8. Consult your physician if symptoms persist.
   a. _____
   b. _____
9. Do not take this product if you are allergic to aspirin or if you have asthma.
   a. _____
   b. _____

B. Each statement is about the expected results of using an item in a medicine cabinet. Change each to a statement with **be supposed to.**

You can expect Seddo sedative not to be very strong.
Seddo sedative isn't supposed to be very strong.

1. You can expect Cressed toothpaste to prevent cavities.
   _____

2. You can expect Endopain painkillers to end discomfort fast.
   _____

3. You can expect Antisep mouthwash not to taste unpleasant.
   _____

4. You can expect Buff headache pills not to affect your stomach.
   _____

27 Modal of obligation and expectation

5. You can expect Nosneeze cold capsules to be effective for 12 hours.
   _____

6. You can expect Pouriton aftershave to smell woodsy.
   _____

7. You can expect Ouchless burn ointment not to get your clothes greasy.
   _____

C. Mark each sentence as **o** (obligation), **e** (expectation), **p** (prohibition), or **n.e.** (negative expectation).

_e_   Is this deodorant supposed to keep you dry for 24 hours?

___ 1. You're not supposed to used these throat lozenges for a persistent cough.

___ 2. I'm not to get more than one refill on this prescription.

___ 3. What are these tablets supposed to be good for?

___ 4. I'm not supposed to have any more problems with stomach distress if I watch my diet and take these pills regularly.

___ 5. Am I to take these before, after, or with meals?

___ 6. An electric razor isn't supposed to give as close a shave as a safety razor.

___ 7. You're supposed to use tranquilizers only if they're prescribed by a doctor.

Vocabulary Summary

affect	deodorant	pain	rinse out
after shave	discomfort	painkiller	sedative
allergic	distress	persist	side effect
aspirin	dose	persistent	stomach
asthma	effective	physician	surface
brush	exceed	pill	symptom
burn	(be) good for	prescribe	tablet
capsule	greasy	prescription	throat
cavity	headache	prevent	toothpaste
cold (in the head)	lozenge	procedure	tranquilizer
	medicine cabinet	razor	
consult	mouthwash	refill	
cough	ointment	relieve	

28 Modals in the past

Mistakes and regrets

Modal auxiliaries with a regular form for expressing the past include **could**, **should/ought to**, **may/might**, and **must** and their negatives. All are followed by **have** + the past participle of the main verb. These past modals commonly express:

1. unrealized ability or possibility

   *Why did I bring so much luggage? I **could have managed** with only one suitcase.*

2. impossibility (surprise)

   *Are you kidding? You **couldn't have brought** four suitcases for a week!*
   *I did, though. Thanks for your help in carrying them. I **couldn't have done** it without you.*

3. unrealized obligation

   *You **should/ought to have told** me I was wearing only one earring.*

4. recognition of a mistake

   *Well, you **shouldn't/ought not to have left** the house without checking in the mirror.*

5. possibility

   *I'm worried. I think I **may/might have left** the oven on. I **may/might not have turned** it off.*

6. conclusion

   *You **must have turned off** the oven. You always check it before you leave. See? I **must not have checked** it this time. It's a good thing we came back.*

*Note: "I could/should/ought to have gone" means "I didn't go."
"I shouldn't/ought not to have gone" means "I went."

These past modals also have progressive forms: modal + **have been** + the -**ing** form of the main verb.

*I **must have been thinking about** other things than earrings and ovens when we left the house.*

28 Modals in the past   96

A. Express regret for things you were able to do but didn't do. Use the idea in each sentence to write another with **could have**.

    I was able to manage with only one suitcase, but I didn't.
    I could have managed with only one suitcase.

1. I was able to go to college right after high school, but I didn't.

2. I was able to buy the same coat on sale by waiting a week, but I didn't.

3. I was able to say something really sarcastic in response, but I didn't.

4. I was able to tell him the truth about how he looked, but I didn't.

B. Express surprise at other people's "mistakes." Use the idea in each sentence to write another with **couldn't have**.

    You brought four suitcases for a week.
    You couldn't have brought four suitcases for a week!

1. You paid $100 for that watch.

2. You saw my name in the newspaper.

3. You were eating without me.

4. You lost the locket I gave you.

C. Express regret for things you didn't do. Use the idea in each sentence to write another with **should have**. Then write it with **ought to have**.

    I didn't check the mirror before leaving the house.
    a. *I should have checked the mirror before leaving the house.*
    b. *I ought to have checked the mirror before leaving the house.*

1. I didn't send my landlady the rent check earlier.
    a.
    b.

2. I didn't let anybody help me wallpaper my kitchen.
    a.
    b.

Modals in the past 28

3. I wasn't trying to save money before I retired.

   a. _____
   b. _____

4. I didn't speak to the neighbors about their noise.

   a. _____
   b. _____

I missed your Anniversary

a. _____
b. _____

D. Express regret for things you did. Use the idea in each sentence to write another with **shouldn't have**. Then write it with **ought not to have**.

   I left the house without checking the mirror.
   a. *I shouldn't have left the house without checking the mirror.*
   b. *I ought not to have left the house without checking the mirror.*

1. I quit my job without having another.

   a. _____
   b. _____

2. I forgot my mother's birthday.

   a. _____
   b. _____

3. I was using your car without your permission.

   a. _____
   b. _____

28 Modals in the past 98

4. I slept for eighteen hours last night.
   a. _____
   b. _____

E. Express possibilities of error. Use the idea in each sentence to write another with **may or may not have**. Then write it with **might or might not have**.

   Maybe I left the oven on.
   a. *I may or may not have left the oven on.*
   b. *I might or might not have left the oven on.*

1. Maybe I misinterpreted what she said.
   a. _____
   b. _____

2. Maybe I put the wrong letter in the envelope.
   a. _____
   b. _____

3. Maybe I swam too far out.
   a. _____
   b. _____

4. Maybe I was eating the wrong things all my life.
   a. _____
   b. _____

F. Express embarrassing conclusions. Use the idea in each sentence to write another with **must** or **must not have**.

   I conclude that I was thinking about something else while you were talking.
   I must have been thinking about something else while you were talking.

1. I conclude that I wasn't concentrating on what you were saying.
   _____

2. I conclude that I was standing in the wrong line for fifteen minutes.
   _____

3. I conclude that I threw away your gift by mistake.
   _____

4. I conclude that I didn't hear the police siren behind me because I had the radio on so loud.
   _____
   _____

Review of modals 29

Study habits and homework

Some of the uses of modal auxiliaries in English are to talk about the following:

1. ability: **can, be able to**

   Can* you/*are* you *able to figure out the answer to the eighth problem?

2. permission: **may, can**

   May/Can I ask you a question about the chemistry homework?

3. customary past: **used to, would**

   When I was younger, I ***didn't use to*** know how to study. ***I'd*** waste a lot of time.

4. customary present: **be used to**

   Now ***I'm used to*** following a regular routine, which makes me a much more efficient student.

5. past intention: **be about to**

   I was about to go to bed when I realized that I hadn't done my English homework yet.

6. obligation/necessity: **have to, must**

   I wouldn't think of putting my English homework off until tomorrow. ***I have to/must*** finish it tonight.

7. desirability/obligation: **should/ought to, had better**

   This writing assignment looks messy. I wonder if I ***should*** copy it over. I probably ***ought to***. In fact, I'm sure ***I'd better*** copy it over; I ***shouldn't*** hand it in looking like this.

8. preference: **would rather, would like**

   I'd rather take the time and effort to copy this than hand it in as it is. ***I'd like*** it to look perfect.

29 Review of modals

> 9. **possibility: can, could, may, might**
>
>   *My answer to #3 **can't** be right. The area of the circle **couldn't** be 1,000,000 square feet. I wonder what I did wrong. I **may/might** be using the wrong formula.*
>
> 10. **probability/inference: should/ought to, must**
>
>   *I was using the wrong formula. There. That **should/ought to** be right now. What's the matter with me? I **must** be losing my mind.*
>
> 11. **obligation and expectation: be supposed to**
>
>   *And I'm **supposed to** be good at math. Oh well... O.K., now what **are** we **supposed to** do in #4?*

A. Fill each blank with **to** or **X** (no **to**).

   I'm sure you can __X__ figure out the answers yourself if you try.

1. Yes, I'm able ___ help you, but I don't think I should.
2. May I ___ look at your answers and see if they're the same as mine?
3. I used ___ have poor study habits.
4. I would ___ use my study time inefficiently.
5. Now I'm used ___ setting aside a certain time for uninterrupted study.
6. I was just about ___ give up on my science assignment when suddenly it began to make sense.
7. Why do we have ___ have homework?
8. You must ___ concentrate when you study.
9. You should ___ have no distractions.
10. You ought ___ be in a quiet room by yourself if possible.
11. I'd better ___ turn off the radio, hadn't I?
12. Is there anyone who would rather ___ study than anything else?
13. As for me, I'd like ___ be at the beach now, not at my desk.
14. That could ___ be why I'm not concentrating on my work very well.
15. I might ___ have to give up for now. It's too hot to think.
16. What were we supposed ___ do for biology homework?

29 Review of modals

B. Change each modal to its negative form. Use contractions where possible. Write both the subject and the modal auxiliary.

he can't	he can
_____	1. we're able to
_____	2. you may
_____	3. they used to
_____	4. I would
_____	5. she's used to
_____	6. they have to
_____	7. you must (obligation/necessity)
_____	8. we should
_____	9. he ought to
_____	10. I'd better
_____	11. they'd rather
_____	12. it could
_____	13. they may
_____	14. you might
_____	15. it must (probability/inference)
_____	16. I'm supposed to

C. Match each sentence with the use of its modal. You will use some items more than once.

---

a. ability
b. inability
c. permission
d. denial of permission
e. customary past*
f. customary present*
g. past intention*
h. obligation/necessity
i. negative obligation
j. prohibition
k. advisability/obligation*
l. preference*
m. possibility*
n. probability*
o. obligation
p. expectation*

* = affirmative or negative

_d_   You may not watch TV until you've finished your homework.
___ 1. This answer can't be right.
___ 2. Are you used to snacking while you study?
___ 3. You have to study hard if you are to succeed.
___ 4. This is supposed to be easy, but it isn't.
___ 5. You mustn't try to do two things at once.

29 Review of modals   102

_____ 6. I can't think of an answer.
_____ 7. You can ask me questions now if you want.
_____ 8. I've gotten several different results, but this one should be right.
_____ 9. You'd better check that answer again.
_____ 10. Can you do #23?
_____ 11. We don't have to do the third exercise; it's optional.
_____ 12. I used to drink a lot of coffee while I studied, until I learned that it slows the thinking process.
_____ 13. What should I do if I can't finish this in time for class?
_____ 14. The teacher didn't say anything about homework for tomorrow, so there must not be any.
_____ 15. You were about to say something when I asked you to be quiet.
_____ 16. Let me see, would I rather do physics or geometry first?
_____ 17. After only six hours, I think I might be finished with my homework.
_____ 18. Are we supposed to write that essay for tomorrow or for Monday?
_____ 19. I must learn this tonight for the quiz tomorrow.

_____ 20. I'm sorry I wasn't able to turn in my homework.
_____ 21. I thought I'd forgotten all the French I used to know last year, but it's beginning to come back this year.
_____ 22. You shouldn't try to read in such a dim light.
_____ 23. I'd rather not study now, but what choice do I have?
_____ 24. I couldn't be finished already, could I?

D. Two English students are on the phone. Rewrite their conversation. Write each underlined sentence in a different way, keeping a similar meaning. Some items have more than one possible answer.

Anders: Let's speak English. <u>It can be good practice for us.</u>
Kiko: All right, I'll try.
Anders: Good. <u>What are we to do for English homework for tomorrow?</u>
Kiko: That's right, you weren't in class today. How come?

29 Review of modals

103

Anders: <u>I couldn't get a ride.</u>
Kiko: Why didn't you call me?
Anders: <u>I was going to</u>, but I didn't want to bother you.
Kiko: <u>You may call me any time.</u> <u>You ought to know that.</u>
Anders: O.K., thanks. Next time I will. In fact, <u>I might need a ride again Tuesday.</u> <u>Can you pick me up then?</u>
Kiko: Sure, no problem. Anyway, the homework. <u>We're supposed to study the modal auxiliaries.</u>
Anders: Oh no <u>Must we?</u> I'd like to do almost anything else. <u>I'm simply not able to understand those modals.</u>
Kiko: <u>They should be easy.</u> We've both been using them all through this conversation
Anders: *Let's speak English.* _____
Kiko: _____
Anders: _____
Kiko: _____
Anders: _____
Kiko: _____
Anders: _____
Kiko: _____
Anders: _____
Kiko: _____
Anders: _____
Kiko: _____

Vocabulary Summary

assignment	essay	inefficiently	regular
biology	exercise	make sense	result
check	figure out	messy	routine
chemistry	formula	optional	set aside
come back	geometry	physics	snack
concentrate	give up	practice	study habits
copy over	give up on	problem	(in) time for
distraction	(be) good at	process	turn in
do homework	hand in	put off	uninterrupted
efficient	homework	quiz	waste

30 Nonseparable two-word verbs

Headlines

> Two-word verbs consist of a verb + a preposition or adverb; together, the two words have a special idiomatic meaning.
>
> Some two-word verbs can be separated by a short direct object: **look over** the newspaper/**look** the newspaper **over**. If the object is a pronoun, the verb **must** be separated: **look it over**.
>
> Other two-word verbs, and all three-word verbs, must **not** be separated by an object: **look into** the story; **look into** it.
>
> Some common nonseparable two- and three-word verbs, with meanings, are listed in the vocabulary summary.

Each newspaper headline contains a two- or three-word verb. Some are separable, some are not. Write each verb with the appropriate pronoun object. (Note: Because headlines must be short, they often omit words that would appear in complete sentences.)

1. **COUPLE BRINGS UP TWELVE FOSTER CHILDREN** _____

2. **Father Is Looking for Long-Lost Daughter** _____

3. **CLASS LOOKS FORWARD TO FORTIETH REUNION** _____

4. **HOMEOWNER WARNS: *KEEP OFF MY PROPERTY*** _____

5. **MAN CHECKED OUT BOOK 27 YEARS AGO; SAYS, "I FORGOT"** _____

6. ***MAYOR PICKS OUT NEW ADVISORS*** _____

30 Nonseparable two-word verbs

7. **Police Looking Into Bizarre Murder** _____

8. *WOMAN COMES ACROSS RARE COIN IN FORGOTTEN BOX* _____

9. **80-YEAR-OLD TAKES UP AEROBIC DANCING** _____

10. ROBBERY VICTIM POINTS OUT THIEF _____

11. *BEGRIMIA TAKES OVER NEIGHBORING COUNTRY* _____

12. Grieving Parents Wonder: *What Has Become of Our Son?* _____

13. PRINCIPAL WARNS STUDENTS: DON'T DROP OUT OF SCHOOL _____

14. *Economists Suggest that Everyone Save up Money for Retirement Now* _____

15. HIGHWAY DEPARTMENT *FINALLY* GETS THROUGH WITH REPAVING _____

16. President Turns Down Husband As Running Mate in Two Years _____

17. GOVERNMENT'S INCOME HASN'T CAUGHT UP WITH OUTGO _____

18. *DRUNK DRIVER RUNS OVER SEVEN NEIGHBORS' LAWNS* _____

19. COMMUNITY ACTIVIST GROUP CALLS FOR ADDITIONAL POLICE _____

30 Nonseparable two-word verbs

20. **ELXON COMPANY PRESIDENT HANDS IN RESIGNATION** _____

21. **MAN BREAKS BOTH LEGS WHILE GETTING OFF TRAIN** _____

22. **Committee to Take up Zoning Issues at Meeting Tuesday** _____

23. **MAYOR DECLARES EMERGENCY: *"WE MUST DO WITHOUT WATER"*** _____

24. **Woman Pays Back Loan After 41 Years; Says, *"I FORGOT"*** _____

Vocabulary Summary

become of -- to happen to
call for -- to request strongly
call on -- to pay a short visit to
catch up with -- to overtake
check up on -- to investigate
come across -- to find by chance
come along with - to accompany
do without -- to sacrifice
drop out of -- to stop attending
get along with -- to cooperate, be congenial
get on; get off -- to board; leave (a plane, train, bus, etc.; not a car)
get over -- to recover from
get through with -- to finish
give up on -- not to attempt any longer
go over -- to review, practice
keep off -- not to go on

keep up with -- to keep pace with
look after -- to take care of
look down on -- to view as inferior
look for -- to try to find
look forward to -- to anticipate
look into -- to investigate
look out for -- to be careful of
look up to -- to admire
put up with -- to tolerate
run across -- to find or meet by chance
run out of -- to use up the supply of
run over -- to hit with a car, etc.
take after -- to resemble
take care of -- to have responsibility for
take charge of -- to take responsibility for
wait on -- to serve

Causative: MAKE, HAVE, GET 31
Goods and services

When someone causes others to do something, we use **make, have,** or **get**. All are followed by objects, then by verb forms. The simple verb form follows **make** and **have**. The infinitive follows **get**.

> *How can I **make them fix** this phone?*
> *I'll **have Sue call** them.*
> *She can **get them to come**!*

Make is used when one person has authority over another. Then it expresses force or pressure.

> *The phone company is trying **to make** me **pay** for calls I didn't make.*

Make is also used to mean simply **cause**, without the sense of authority. With this meaning, it may be followed by an adjective or a verb.

> *The phone company **is making** me **furious**; they're **making** me **act** irrationally.*

Have is used in situations of authority, but it is softer than **make**. It is often used when one person employs another.

> *When I go to the Hair Place, I usually **have** Betty **do** my hair.*

Get expresses persuasion. Notice the infinitive.

> *I hope I can **get** Betty **to do** my hair this Friday.*

Have and **get** can also be followed by passive forms, with non-human objects + a past participle.

> *I usually **have** my hair **done** by Betty, at The Hair Place.*
> *I hope I can **get** my hair **done** by Betty this Friday.*

A. Fill in each blank with a form of <u>make</u> (meaning "force") or <u>get</u>.

I wish I could _make_ the electric company believe that I don't owe them for the last three months.

1. I can't seem to _____ them to listen to me.
2. The problem is that they're trying to _____ computers do the work of human beings, and there's no way to _____ a computer to respond with sympathy.

31 Causative: MAKE, HAVE, GET

3. How do you _____ something done by talking to a computer?
4. The whole thing is _____ me extremely irritated.
5. Yesterday I _____ my suit drycleaned at Kwik-Kleen.
6. It used to be blue, but somehow they managed to _____ it turn gray.
7. After I go down there and _____ them pay me for a new suit, nothing will ever _____ me to go back to Kwik-Kleen again.

B. Rewrite each advertising claim with a form of <u>make</u> (meaning "cause").

Your spots and stains will disappear fast if you use Solvo rug cleaner.
<u>Solvo rug cleaner will make your spots and stains disappear fast!</u>

1. Your teeth will be whiter if you use Brite toothpaste.
   _____
   _____

2. You'll be able to sleep like a baby if you take Sleepade.
   _____
   _____

3. Your flowers will grow twice as fast if you buy Bloomalot.
   _____
   _____

4. Your wrinkles will disappear if you use Teen Creme.
   _____
   _____

5. Your dishes will be spotless if you use Seethru detergent.
   _____
   _____

31 Causative: MAKE, HAVE, GET

C. Last week, Mrs. Armbruster took her car to a garage for service. This is her list of what she had them do. For each item on the list, write one active sentence and one passive sentence with <u>had</u>. Add necessary articles.

> **NOTES**
> Bud, on my car, please —
> 1. adjust brakes
> 2. change snow tires
> 3. fix clutch
> 4. check oil
> 5. wash and wax car
> 6. fill gas tank
> 7. replace battery
> 8. change air filter
>   thanks, Mia
>   *Mia Armbruster*

1. a. _____
   b. _____
2. a. _____
   b. _____
3. a. _____
   b. _____
4. a. _____
   b. _____
5. a. _____
   b. _____
6. a. _____
   b. _____
7. a. _____
   b. _____
8. a. _____
   b. _____

31 Causative: MAKE, HAVE, GET

D. Mr. D'Amato is having his apartment fixed up. Use the words in parentheses to write sentences about what he's getting done.

1. (clean - carpets)
   _____

2. (paint - walls)
   _____

3. (reupholster - couch and chair)
   _____

4. (replace - stove)
   _____

5. (wash - windows)
   _____

6. (install - new locks)
   _____

7. (dye - curtains)
   _____

8. (put in - air conditioning)
   _____

Vocabulary Summary

adjust	dryclean	interior	services
air filter	dye	irrational	snow tire
authority	electric company	irritated	spot
battery	fix	oil	spotless
brake	furious	owe	stain
carpet	garage	phone company	sympathy
clutch (of a car)	gas tank	put in	toothpaste
detergent	goods	replace	wax
disappear	install	reupholster	wrinkle

Passive voice I

Sciences

> We form the passive with **be** + the past participle of the main verb.
>
> 1. simple present
>
>   *Water **is made up of** two parts hydrogen to one part oxygen.*
>
> 2. present progressive
>
>   *Important experiments **are being carried on** in this lab 24 hours a day.*
>
> 3. future
>
>   *A scientific breakthrough **will be/is going to be announced** within a week.*
>
> 4. with modals
>
>   *An atom **can't be seen** by the naked eye.*
>
> We use the passive
>
> 1. with **by** + an agent (a noun or noun phrase) unless the agent is unknown or unimportant to understanding the sentence:
>
>   *The movement of the Earth's crust **is being studied by geologists** around the world.*
>   *It is now thought that many mental illnesses **are caused by chemical imbalance** in the body.*
>   *Cures for cancer **are being sought** all over the world.*
>
> 2. especially in formal writing, technical reports, news articles, etc.

A. Change each sentence from active to passive. Include the agent.

Friction creates heat.
Heat is created by friction.

1. A laser beam can burn a hole in a steel plate.

   _____

32 Passive voice I

2. A prism will separate "white" light into a rainbow pattern, or spectrum.

3. Electron tubes and transistors generate radio waves.

4. Astronomers all over the world are now using radio telescopes to study distant stars.

5. Our eyes can detect light waves, but no one can see radio and television waves. (Change two verbs.)

6. Contact with the earth weakens surface radio waves.

7. Using air gives power to a gasoline engine.

8. Gravity restricts the mobility of vehicles on earth.

9. Every consumer should study statistics and how unscrupulous people might manipulate them. (Change two verbs.)

B. Change each sentence from active to passive. Omit the agent.

1. You can divide the physical sciences into the two main divisions of chemistry and physics.

2. Now more than ever before, people need large amounts of inexpensive energy.

3. Doctors are treating some cancer conditions with lasers.

4. In stereophonic sound, we receive sounds from two or more separate areas.

5. People may yet discover more planets.

113   Passive voice I **32**

6. You must amplify a weak radio signal.
    _____

7. We call the atmosphere above 25 miles the ionosphere.
    _____

8. Someday, they will build communities in space.
    _____

9. In space, they are navigating a craft in earth orbit.
    _____

10. It's easy for someone to mislead you about the meaning of a statistical "average."
    _____
    _____

C. Rewrite this paragraph using the passive wherever possible and omitting the agents when they are unnecessary.

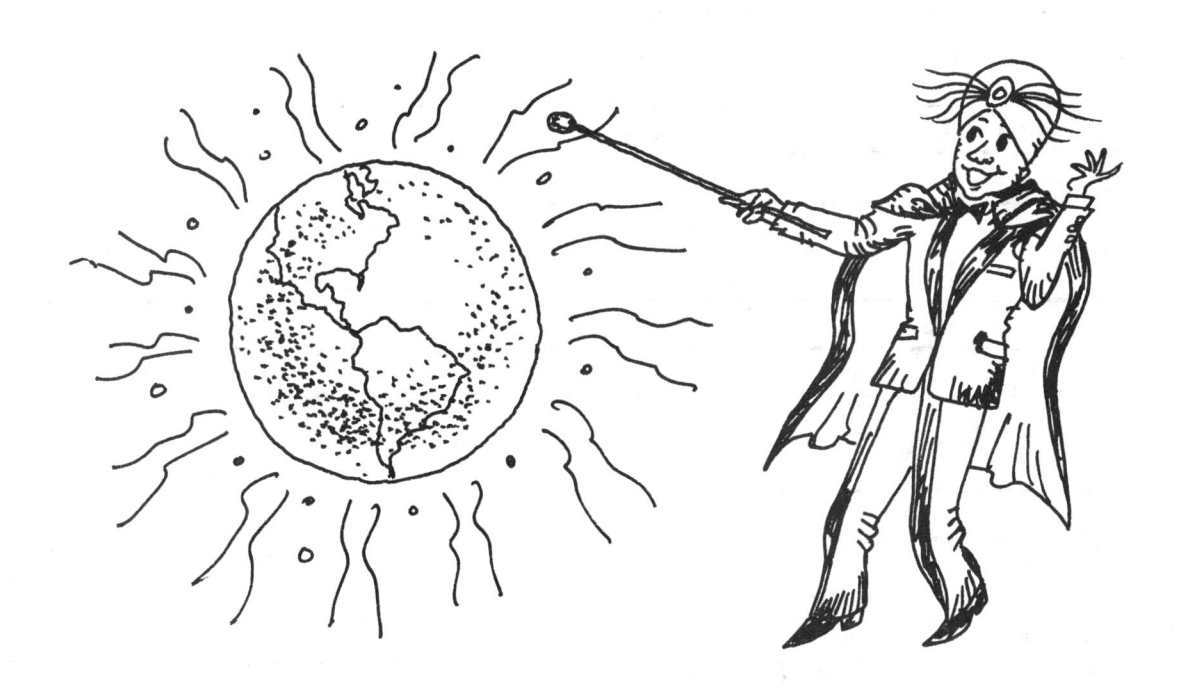

A Prediction

　　We will make great breakthroughs in science in the next few years. We are going to understand much more about the history of the Earth and the way forces under its crust change it. People will also learn a lot more about the stars.

32 Passive voice I

Researchers around the world are going to understand the origins of the universe and of life. Not all scientists will accept the answers to these mysteries, but those who don't believe in astrophysics and biological evolution will become less important. Who will make the wonderful scientific discoveries of the future? The Einsteins and Darwins of the next century may be studying in our grade schools today -- in Brisbane or Hofuf, in Chongqing, Santiago, or Lagos. We know nothing about them now; they are faceless nobodies. However, we can predict this with certainty: the next generation will change the world.

Great breakthroughs

Vocabulary Summary

amplify	detect	lab	signal
astronomer	electron	laser	sought
atmosphere	energy	(be) made up of	spectrum
atom	engine	movement	statistical
breakthrough	experiment	navigate	statistics
cancer	friction	orbit	stereophonic
carry on	geologist	oxygen	telescope
chemical	gravity	planet	transistor
consumer	hydrogen	power	treat
crust	imbalance	prism	tube
cure	ionosphere	scientific	wave

Passive voice II 33

Disease

We form the passive with **be** + the past participles of the main verb.

1. simple past

    *Polio vaccine **was developed** by Jonas Salk.*

2. past progressive

    *Until then, various other methods, some very painful, **were being used** to combat polio.*

Note: The progressive forms of perfect tenses are not used in passive.

3. perfect

    *In recent years, great strides **have been made** in eradicating smallpox.*

4. past perfect

    *Countless victims **had been attacked** by smallpox before a cure was discovered.*

5. with modals

    *Something **had to be done**.*

We use the passive

1. with **by** (sometimes **with**) + an agent (a noun or noun phrase) unless the agent is unknown, or unimportant to understanding the sentence:

    *Vaccination against smallpox **was first tried by Louis Pasteur**.*
    *Thousands, perhaps millions, of people **were killed by the Black Death**, or bubonic plague, in the fourteenth century. Nothing like it **has been seen** since.*

2. especially in formal writing, technical reports, news articles, etc.

33 Passive voice II 116

A. Change each sentence from active to passive. Include the agent.

Horace Wells first used anesthesia in his dental practice.

Anesthesia was first used by Horace Wells in his dental practice.

1. The use of drugs has extended the lives of children with leukemia to as much as ten years.

2. Observation had detected the woman's skin cancer before a biopsy confirmed it. (Change two verbs.)

3. Someone whom an insect has stung can have a severe allergic reaction.

4. By the end of 1918, an influenza epidemic had killed an estimated 20,000,000 people worldwide.

5. In 1977, they found that a bacterium caused "legionnaire's disease."

6. Takamine discovered adrenalin in 1901.

7. Von Behring won the first Nobel Prize in Medicine.

8. Pasteur developed the germ theory of disease, established the principle of immunity, and originated inoculation. (Change three verbs.)

9. Since Galton discovered ultrasound over 60 years ago, medical science has used it in various ways. (Change two verbs.)

B. Change each sentence from active to passive. Omit the agent.

They were using anesthesia as early as 1842.
Anesthesia was being used as early as 1842.

1. They could have cured your throat cancer before it spread.

2. You were supposed to treat the victim for shock.

3. They were about to pronounce the man drunk when they identified him as diabetic.   (Change two verbs.)

4. Someone first described bacteria in 1676.

33 Passive voice II 118

5. They've given the Nobel Prize in Physiology or Medicine since 1901.
   _____
   _____

6. People had preserved in Arabic the medical knowledge of the ancient Greeks, and then they added contributions from scientists of the Arabic Empire. (Change two verbs.)
   _____
   _____

7. Since the discovery of DNA, people have studied and argued about the possibilities of genetic engineering. (Change two verbs.)
   _____
   _____

8. They have developed two ultrasonic techniques: A-scan and B-scan.
   _____
   _____

9. Ultrasound surpasses X-rays in searching for stones that something has formed in the body.
   _____
   _____

Vocabulary Summary

adrenalin	DNA	leukemia	(make) strides
allergic	drugs	Nobel Prize	technique
anesthesia	epidemic	observation	theory
bacteria	eradicate	painful	treat
bacterium	genetic	physiology	ultrasonic
biopsy	engineering	plague	ultrasound
combat	germ	polio	vaccine
cure	immunity	practice	victim
detect	influenza	reaction	X-ray
develop	inoculation	shock	
diabetic	legionnaire's	smallpox	
disease	disease	stone	

Gerunds 34

Exercise

> A gerund is a verb form ending in **-ing**, used as a noun.
> There are three principal uses of the gerund:
>
> 1. as direct object
>
>   *The downstairs neighbors don't like my* **doing** push ups at 4 a.m.*
>
> *A noun or pronoun before a gerund is possessive.
>
> 2. as subject of a clause or sentence
>
>   *If **swimming** is such good exercise, how come whales have so much blubber?*
>
> 3. as object of a preposition
>
>   *I'm worn out from **lifting** weights.*

A. Write the sentences with gerund forms of the verbs in parentheses.

Do you believe in (get) a lot of exercise?
Do you believe in getting a lot of exercise?

1. I'd work on (build) muscles, but I don't have any weights.

2. I know I should exercise more, but I don't care for (do) anything very strenuous.

3. Why does everyone laugh at my (plan) to climb Mount Everest in three hours?

4. I like my doctor. She doesn't approve of anyone's (work out) with fancy equipment.

5. Exercising to build muscles is very different from (exercise) for health.

34 Gerunds   120

6. Thank you for (hold) my feet while I did my sit ups; I couldn't have done even one without you.
   _____
   _____

7. While all of you do calisthenics, I'll be in charge of (count).
   _____
   _____

8. I go to the gym because in addition to (want) to lose some weight, I'm interested in (strengthen) my muscles.
   _____
   _____

9. I refuse to exercise for fear of (end up) in worse shape than I'm in now.
   _____
   _____

B. Rewrite each sentence with a gerund as subject.

It's good for everyone to get moderate exercise every day.
Getting moderate exercise everyday is good for everyone.

1. It's dangerous to overdo it, though.
   _____
   _____

2. It's best to begin slowly and gradually build up the amount of effort you make. (Change two verb.)
   _____
   _____

3. It can be beneficial to your work to take an exercise break during the day.
   _____
   _____

4. It makes me tired to go through my exercise routine, but it's worth it to do so. (Change two verbs.)
   _____
   _____

5. It's more helpful to work out with someone else than it is to do it alone. (Change two verbs.)
   _____
   _____

Gerunds **34**

6. If it makes you embarrassed to go to the gym with your physique, it's possible to accomplish a lot right at home. (Change two verbs.)

   _____

   _____

7. It's tempting to quit jogging, but it's correspondingly shocking to remember the condition I was in before I started. (Change two verbs.)

   _____

   _____

GYM SCENE

a. climb a rope
b. do sit ups
c. do push ups
d. work out on the rings
e. do chin ups
f. lift weights
g. ride an exercycle
h. play basketball

34 Gerunds

C. Complete the sentences about the activities above.

I enjoy _exercising_.
Exercising is enjoyable.
I'm worn out from _exercising_.

1. I enjoy _____.
   _____ is enjoyable.
   I'm tired out from _____.

2. I enjoy _____.
   _____ is enjoyable.
   I'm exhausted from _____.

3. I enjoy _____.
   _____ is enjoyable.
   I'm fatigued from _____.

4. I enjoy _____.
   _____ is enjoyable.
   I'm done in from _____.

5. I enjoy _____.
   _____ is enjoyable.
   I'm bushed from _____.

6. I enjoy _____.
   _____ is enjoyable.
   I'm beat from _____.

7. I enjoy _____.
   _____ is enjoyable.
   I'm dog-tired from _____.

8. I enjoy _____.
   _____ in enjoyable.
   I'm tuckered out from _____.

Vocabulary Summary

beneficial	gym	overdo	take a break
build up	jog	physique	weights
calisthenics	lift weights	push up (n.)	work on
climb	lose weight	routine	work out
condition	make (someone)	(be in) shape	(be) worn out
effort	tired	sit up (n.)	(from)
equipment	moderate	strenuous	(be) worth it
exercise	muscle	swim	

Verb + gerund 35

A life of crime

A gerund is a verb form ending in **-ing** that functions as a noun.

*"**Stealing** is fun,"* says Butch. (gerund subject)
*"I really **enjoy taking** beautiful things."* (gerund object)

Use **not** for a negative gerund:

*Butch's parents regret **not punishing** him when he was a child.*

A noun or pronoun before a gerund is possessive:

*Algernon really minds his **brother's being** a crook.*

The following verbs take gerund objects; they are not followed by infinitives (see Lesson 36).

acknowledge	get through	quit
admit	give up	recall
appreciate	imagine	regret
avoid	keep (continue)	resent
can't help	keep on	resist
consider	mind	risk
deny	miss	stop (quit)
enjoy	postpone	suggest
finish	practice	understand

Combine the opening and the sentence into one sentence with a gerund object. Don't use the negative in your sentence.

Butch acknowledges...He stole Mrs. Van Clee's emerald brooch.
Butch acknowledges stealing Mrs. Van Clee's emerald brooch.

1. He admits...He sold the brooch to pay off an illegal bet.

35 Verb + gerund 124

2. Mrs. Van Clee didn't appreciate...She lost her brooch.

3. Now she avoids...She (doesn't) go to dinner parties where she would have worn it.

4. Butch can't seem to help...He's a criminal.

5. He won't consider...He (won't) lead any other kind of life.

6. However, Butch denies...He (never) hurt anyone while committing a robbery.

7. Butch enjoys...He breaks and enters for the excitement of being in someone else's house.

8. He'll finish...He serves his jail sentence in three years, with time off for good behavior.

9. He'll be glad to see the light of day again when he gets through...He's doing time.

10. Butch's sister, Mae, used to be a thief, too. She's given up...She (doesn't) steal since she got married.

11. Now she can't imagine...She (won't) break into someone's house.

12. However, Mae's husband, Dutch, keeps...He cracks safes.

Verb + gerund

13. Dutch will probably keep on...He'll be a safecracker until he loses his touch.

14. Mae doesn't mind...She has a safecracker for a husband.

15. When Dutch retires, Mae will miss...She gets nice surprise presents from him.

16. Dutch was going to go out on a job tonight, but he postponed...He (isn't) going because he's coming down with a cold.

17. Instead, he'll stay home to practice...He'll find safe combinations on his collection in the basement.

18. Mae and Butch have a younger brother named Algernon. He didn't have to quit...He (doesn't) live a life of crime, because they taught him differently.

35 Verb + gerund   126

19. Mae and Butch recall...They taught Algernon to be the good one in the family.
    _____
    _____

20. They don't regret...They told him that crime doesn't pay in the end.
    _____
    _____

21. Algernon used to resent...He was the baby in the family, and the only "different" one.
    _____
    _____

22. He used to beg to be taken along on a job, but Butch and Mae resisted...They (wouldn't) take him.
    _____
    _____

23. They didn't want to risk...They (didn't want) to lose their baby brother.
    _____
    _____

24. Algernon wishes Butch would stop...He hangs out with burglars, thieves, and robbers.
    _____
    _____

25. In conversations with Butch, Algernon has often suggested...He wants him** to reform.
    _____
    _____

26. Algernon can't understand...Butch** associates with known criminals. Algernon forgets that Butch is in prison and doesn't have much choice.
    _____
    _____

** Use a possessive.

Vocabulary Summary

bet	commit	jail	safecracker
break into	crack a safe	job	sentence
breaking and entering	crime	lose one's touch	serve
	criminal	pay off	steal
brooch	crook	reform	thief
burglar	good behavior	robber	(do) time
combination (of a safe)	hang out with	robbery	time off
	illegal	safe (n.)	

Verb + infinitive 36

Teachers

All the verbs in this lesson can be followed by infinitives but do not take gerund objects (see lesson 35).

1. These verbs are followed by infinitives + objects (if any), in that order.

agree	consent	forget	manage	seem
appear	decide	happen	offer	tend
arrange	deserve	hope	plan	try
care*	desire	learn	refuse	

   *Ha! The teacher **forgot to give** us homework!*

   ***Care** appears in the negative or in questions.*

2. These verbs are followed by objects + infinitives, in that order. The object is necessary in active sentences.

advise	convince	hire	persuade	urge
allow	encourage	instruct	remind	warn*
authorize	forbid	invite	request	
cause	force	oblige	teach	
challenge	get	order	tell	
command	help	permit	train	

   *She didn't **remind us to bring** our workbooks to class tomorrow, either.*

   ***Warn** is usually followed by **not** + an object and an infinitive.*

   Most of these verbs can be used in passive without a change in meaning:

   *Someone **hired me to teach**, not to enforce discipline.* (active)
   *I **was hired to teach**, not to enforce discipline.* (passive)

3. These verbs are used with infinitives (pattern 1 above) **or** with objects + infinitives (pattern 2).

ask	expect	prepare	want
beg	need	promise*	would like

   Teacher: *Would you like to help me hand out these papers?*
   Student: *Sure, I'd be glad to.*

   Student: *Would you like me to help you grade the exams?*
   Teacher: *No, thank you. I think I can do it myself.*

36 Verb + infinitive   128

> ***Promise** is different from the other verbs in this list.
>
> *The teacher asked to help; therefore she will probably help.*
> *The teacher asked me to help; therefore I will probably help.*
>
> *The teacher promised to help; therefore she will probably help.*
> *The teacher promised me to help; therefore she will probably help (me).*

A. Study the verbs in the introduction. Then put each verb in the correct column. Try not to look back at the lists.

hired	asked	seemed	hoped	ordered
taught	advised	encouraged	prepared	commanded
planned	invited	refused	told	promised
expected	would like	needed	begged	tried
agreed	managed	decided	wanted	

1	2	3
infinitive only	object and infinitive	either 1 or 2
The teacher **agreed** to give us a day off.	The teacher **advised** us not to take a day off.	The teacher **wants** to take a day off.
	hired	or
		The teacher **wants** us to take a day off.

Verb + infinitive   36

B. Cross out the passive constructions that are not possible in English.

1. I was authorized to...
2. ~~I was forgotten to...~~
3. I was reminded to...
4. I was forced to...
5. I was arranged to...
6. I was learned to...
7. I was consented to...
8. I was trained to...
9. I was instructed to...
10. I was happened to...
11. I was persuaded to...
12. I was appeared to...
13. I was urged to...
14. I was managed to...
15. I was warned to...
16. I was permitted to...

C. Some words are missing from these paragraphs. Rewrite the paragraphs, adding **to** for necessary infinitive forms and **us** for necessary objects.

I'll never understand teachers. Sometimes they seem know everything, but other times they refuse answer questions. They tell figure out the answers ourselves. They say that's because they want try to develop our own thinking processes, but I suspect it's because they aren't sure of the answers.

Sometimes they're dictatorial. They command do this, they order do that, they forbid do something else. Other times, they're more considerate of our feelings. Then

36 Verb + infinitive 130

they ask or request do things, they encourage do our best, and they offer help. They allow make mistakes, and that way they teach learn for ourselves.

Even though I don't understand them, I expect be a teacher someday. I hope be the helpful kind, not the dictatorial kind. Students deserve have the best!

I'll never understand teachers.

Vocabulary Summary

considerate	exam	hand out	take time off
dictatorial	figure out	helpful	thinking process
discipline	forgetful	hire	workbook
enforce	grade (v.)	principal	

37 Verb + gerund or infinitive

Hobbies

These verbs may be followed by either gerunds or infinitives. The meaning is the same.

(can/can't) afford	dislike	like	prefer
(can't) bear	dread	love	(can't) stand
begin	hate	neglect	start
continue	intend	plan (on)*	

*Right now I **can't afford adding** any more stamps to my collection.*
*Right now I **can't afford to add** any more stamps to my collection.*

*Use an infinitive after **plan**. Use a gerund after **plan on**.

*Les **plans to work** in his darkroom all weekend.*
*Les **plans on working** in his darkroom all weekend.*

Allow and **permit** may be followed by gerunds or by objects + infinitives (in that order).

*The laws here **don't allow/permit conducting** a for-profit hobby in a private home.*
*The laws here **don't allow/permit anyone to conduct** a for-profit hobby in a private home.*

Forget and **remember** may be followed by either gerunds or infinitives, but with a difference in meaning.

I didn't remember picking up that coin for my collection.
(I got the coin, but didn't remember the action.)
I didn't remember to pick up that coin for my collection.
(I forgot to get the coin.)

Stop also may be followed by either gerunds or infinitives, but with a difference in meaning.

I've stopped practicing karate at Kim's Martial Arts Studio.
(I don't practice karate there anymore.)
I've stopped to practice karate at Kim's Martial Arts Studio.
(I have visited the studio in order to practice karate.)

37 Verb + gerund or infinitive 132

A. Write the sentences using the verbs in parentheses, first as gerunds, then as infinitives.

What hobby do you intend (take up)?
- a. *What hobby do you intend taking up?*
- b. *What hobby do you intend to take up?*

1. I dread (see) my bills for photographic supplies.
   - a. _____
   - b. _____

2. When did you begin (collect) butterflies?
   - a. _____
   - b. _____

3. I've always liked (fish), but I've always hated (clean) the fish afterward.
   - a. _____
   - b. _____

4. Do you prefer (have) sedentary hobbies or (be) more active?
   - a. _____
   - b. _____

5. I can't stand (be) interrupted when I'm looking at my collection of post cards.
   - a. _____
   - b. _____

6. I've decided that I'm going to start (refinish) this old desk soon.
   - a. _____
   - b. _____

7. I used to enjoy hunting, but I couldn't continue (do) it after I got arthritis in my legs.
   - a. _____
   - b. _____

8. Well, I never wanted to hunt or fish because I couldn't bear (kill) anything.
   - a. _____
   - b. _____

9. Some people love (work on) model airplanes.
   - a. _____
   - b. _____

Verb + gerund or infinitive   37

B. Match each sentence with the correct interpretation.

_c_ 1. My wife doesn't allow me to do my woodworking in the living room.

___ 2. I stopped restoring antique cars when I ran out of money.

___ 3. I stopped work to restore antique cars.

___ 4. I didn't remember to get Liz's autograph for my collection.

___ 5. I didn't remember getting Liz's autograph for my collection.

___ 6. I forgot to get the new butterfly stamps.

___ 7. I forgot getting the new butterfly stamps.

a. I don't restore antique cars.

b. I don't have Liz's autograph.

c. I don't do woodworking in the living room.

d. I have the new stamps.

e. I have Liz's autograph.

f. I don't have the new stamps.

g. I restore antique cars.

37 Verb + gerund or infinitive 134

C. To review verbs and gerunds, infinitives, or either (lessons 35, 36, 37), put each of these verbs in the correct column.

miss	admit	tell	want	can't stand
enjoy	decide	regret	learn	quit
ask	persuade	can't bear	prefer	can't help
start	expect	give up	hope	finish
advise	continue	hate	intend	begin
dislike	love	suggest	manage	force

1
gerunds only
example: **mind**

miss

2
infinitives only
(with or without objects)
examples: **deserve, get, would like**

3
gerunds or infinitives
example: **dread**

Vocabulary Summary

active	darkroom	model	stamp
antique	fishing	photographic	supply
autograph	for-profit	pick up	take up
butterfly	hobby	post card	woodworking
coin	hunting	refinish	
collect	karate	restore	
collection	label	sedentary	

135 Verb + simple or progressive   38
Private eye (P.I.)

> See Lesson 31 for the causative: **have** or **make** + an object + the simple form of a verb.
>
> *Benjamin **is having** a private eye **look for** his former business partner.*
> *He hopes to **make** him **pay back** the money he embezzled from the company.*
>
> **Let** and **help** are also followed by an object + a simple verb form.
>
> *Benjamin doesn't intend **to let** his former partner **escape**.*
> *The detective **is going to help** Benjamin **find** him.*
>
> Certain verbs of perception may be followed by either simple or progressive forms: **feel, hear, see** and **watch**. Use the simple form for a momentary action. Use the progressive form for a continuing action.
>
> *His partner took the money. + Benjamin didn't see him. =*
> *Benjamin **didn't see** his partner **take** the money.*
>
> *He was walking toward the elevator early that day. + However, Benjamin did see him. =*
> *However, Benjamin **did see** him **walking** toward the elevator early that day.*
>
> Other verbs of perception are usually followed by progressive forms: **listen to, look at, notice, observe,** and **overhear**.
>
> *Benjamin got suspicious of his partner when he **overheard** him **making** reservations for a flight to Greenland.*

A. Combine each pair of sentences into one.

Nothing is happening. Sometimes private investigators spend a lot of time looking at it.

Sometimes private investigators spend a lot of time looking at nothing happening.

1. People talk too freely. They often get information just listening to them.

___

38 Verb + simple or progressive forms 136

2. One person made an indiscreet phone call. Fred Shott, P.I., solved a case by hearing her.

3. She was acting suspiciously. Her husband had noticed her.

4. He wanted to get information. He hired Shott to help him.

5. Shott needed to have a lot of information about her habits. The husband let him.

6. The wife left the house one day. Shott saw her.

7. She was walking toward a phone booth. Shott was following her and observed her.

8. She was talking to someone. At first Shott watched her.

9. She was making plans to meet someone. Then he crossed the street and overheard her.

10. He was listening to her. She must have felt him, because she quickly hung up.

11. There were some children playing across the street. She pretended she was looking at them.

12. She was planning a surprise birthday party for her husband. But Shott had heard her.

13. Her husband didn't find out about the party beforehand. Shott kept the secret and didn't let him.

137 Verb + simple or progressive forms 38

B. Rewrite the paragraph about a private eye's experience. Use **felt, heard, saw,** and **watched.**

The suspect entered a video game arcade. I followed him. He asked the attendant for change. He said he needed $5 worth of quarters. He went over to one of the games. He put quarters in the machine and began playing. Soon the machine was making a cacophony of electronic beeps. He played for a few minutes. I became entranced and forgot to keep alert for trouble. Suddenly something hard was poking me in the ribs. A deep voice said not to move or else. I reached for my gun. Something crashed down on my skull. When I came to, both men were gone.

I watched the suspect enter a video game arcade.

C. Unscramble these sentences about the scene on the next page.

1. the little girl/the policeman/along the sidewalk/is watching/walk
   The little girl

2. behind her/she doesn't notice/standing/the two men

3. is looking at/standing by the sign/the dog/the little girl

4. make the drop/the policeman/the two men/see/doesn't

5. is observing/the woman/exchanging/the two men/something

6. talking/Fred Shott/the two men/overhears

38 Verb + simple or progressive forms 138

7. Fred/one of the men/him/watching/feels

Vocabulary Summary

alert	detective	indiscreet	private eye
briefcase	embezzle	information	secret
case	escape	investigator	solve
come to (regain consciousness)	gun	keep a secret	suspect
	habits	partner	suspicious

39 Do vs. Make

Entertaining guests

Do sometimes has the idea of **accomplish**, and **make** sometimes has the idea of **build** or **create**. However, it is best to learn specific phrases or idioms in which each verb appears. For example:

do	make
a job	a meal
homework	a dish (a cake, a casserole, etc.)
exercises	a mistake
dishes	money
housework (also windows, the dusting, etc.)	a speech
	a living
one's best	an appointment
a favor	a bed
laundry	sense
the cooking	an excuse
the shopping	plans/preparations
an assignment	a difference
do without (manage without)	make up one's mind (decide)
do away with (get rid of)	make up (invent)
do over (redecorate)	make up with (become friendly again)
do in (exhaust, kill)	make fun of (ridicule)
do well, badly, etc. (fare)	make out well, badly, etc. (fare)

39   Do vs. Make

A. Bettina and Herb Carlson have invited the Coreys for the weekend. These are some of the things they have to do before their guests arrive.

1. the dusting
2. invent the menus
3. the shopping
4. the guest bed
5. plans for entertainment
6. the best dishes
7. some of the food ahead of time
8. the laundry
9. redecorate the guest room
10. decide whether to invite anyone else

Using the above list, write sentences about what the Carlsons have to do. Begin with "They have to..."

1. _____
2. _____
3. _____
4. _____
5. _____
6. _____
7. _____
8. _____
9. _____
10. _____

Do vs. MAKE 39

B. These are some of the things the Carlsons say while they are getting ready for their guests. Fill in each blank with a form of **do** or **make**. Try not to look back at the lists in the introduction.

1. BRC: Could you help me _____ the guest bed now?
   HJC: As soon as I finish _____ these dishes.
2. BRC: Should we _____ the dusting now?
   HJC: It doesn't _____ sense to _____ it until after we've _____ the vacuuming.
3. HJC: How did the Coreys _____ their money, anyway?
   BRC: They inherited it. Neither of them has ever had to _____ a living.
4. BRC: I shouldn't have _____ my exercises this morning. I'm stiff.
   HJC: Are you _____ excuses for not helping me with this?
   BRC: Are you trying to _____ me in? Tomorrow I'll have to _____ an appointment with the chiropractor.
5. HJC: How are you _____ with the laundry?
   BRC: I'm _____ out O.K. I should have it _____ in half an hour or so.
6. BRC: Could you _____ me a favor? Go get some milk? We've run out, and we really can't _____ without it.
   HJC: Sure, but could you wait until I've finished _____ this salad?
7. HJC: They must have _____ a mistake in this recipe. It calls for a cup of vinegar.
8. HJC: Who's going to _____ dinner tonight?
   BRC: It doesn't _____ any difference to me. Oh, wait -- I forgot. Harvey said he'd _____ it after he _____ his homework. He has to _____ a speech in his English class tomorrow.
   HJC: We _____ a good job with that boy, didn't we?
   BRC: Well, we _____ our best. He turned out O.K.
9. HJC: I hadn't realized there was so much housework to _____.
   BRC: We'd better give up on _____ over the guest room. There won't be time.
10. HJC: Couldn't we _____ away with this lamp? It doesn't work, and it's just in the way.
    BRC: Yesterday you said you wanted to keep it. I wish you'd _____ up your mind.
    HJC: Come on, don't _____ fun of me. And let's not argue.
    BRC: But _____ up with each other afterward is such fun!

39 Do vs. MAKE   142

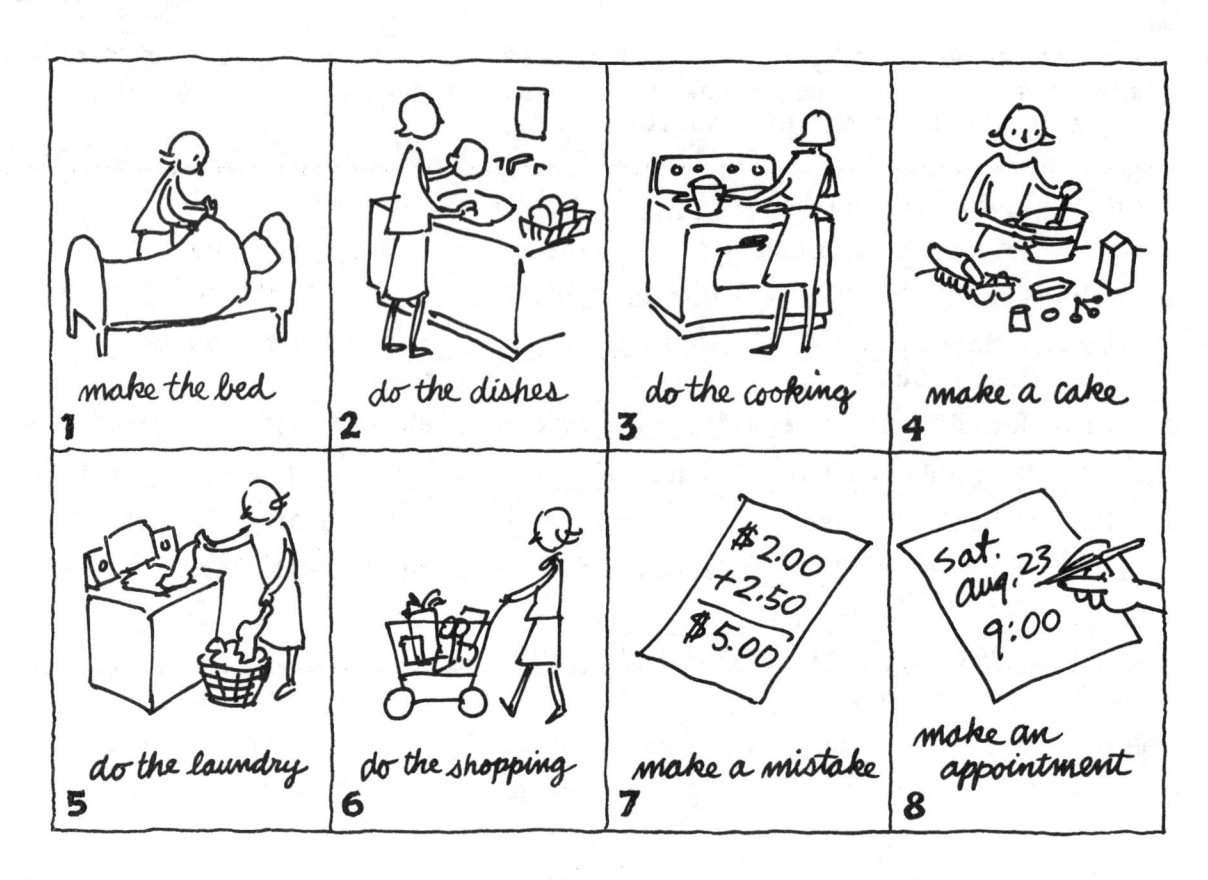

1. make the bed	2. do the dishes	3. do the cooking	4. make a cake
5. do the laundry	6. do the shopping	7. make a mistake	8. make an appointment

CHART

C. Use the chart above and complete the sentence with the correct form of **do** or **make**.

1. Would you _____?
2. It's time to _____.
3. Who's _____?
4. Are you going to _____ for my birthday?
5. We _____ every Saturday.
6. I _____ yesterday.
7. Waiter! You've _____.
8. I want to _____ with you.

Participles as adjectives

Plays

> Both present (**-ing**) and past (**-ed** for regular verbs) participles can function as adjectives. As adjectives, they can be modified by adverbs of degree such as **very**.
>
> The **-ing** form is active. It generally describes a thing:
>
> *Most audiences have thought **A Chorus Line** was a very **exciting** musical.*
>
> The **-ed** form is passive. It generally describes a person:
>
> *In fact, many audiences have been so **excited** about the musical that they've given it standing ovations.*

A. Form the present and past participles of the verbs in this list. Remember to omit a final silent **e**.

amaze _____   horrify _____
amuse _____   interest _____
bore _____   intrigue _____
convince _____   overwhelm _____
depress _____   satisfy _____
disappoint _____   shock _____
disgust _____   surprise _____
excite _____   terrify _____
exhaust _____   thrill _____
fascinate _____   tire _____

40 Participles as adjectives (-ING vs. -ED)   144

B. Fill in each blank with the **–ing** or **–ed** form of the verb in parentheses.

That was one of the most _thrilling_ performances I've ever seen! (thrill)

1. Did you find the play _____ ? (amuse)
2. Audiences were _____ at early performances of Ibsen's plays. (shock)
3. O'Neill's plays are so long that people often find them _____ even though the characters are _____ . (tire, fascinate)
4. I was _____ by the first act, but the second and third acts were much more _____ . (bore, interest)
5. Many people are _____ by the graphic scenes in <u>Sweeney Todd</u>. (disgust)
6. I was _____ by Olivier's Hamlet; it was a completely _____ portrayal. (overwhelm, convince)
7. Were you _____ at the ending of <u>Deathtrap</u>? (surprise)
8. Acting must be one of the most _____ occupations there is. (exhaust)
9. Classical Greek dramas are still _____ to audiences; many people are _____ upon recognizing themselves in the characters. (horrify, terrify)
10. The last play I saw had an _____ plot, but I was _____ in the acting and the scenery. (intrigue, disappoint)
11. Weren't you _____ at what happened in the second scene? (amaze)
12. My reaction to the play was peculiar: I was _____ during it and _____ after it. (excite, depress)
13. Shakespeare's comedies still stand as some of the most _____ ones ever written. (satisfy)

Vocabulary Summary

act	comedy	make-up	portrayal
acting	costumes	musical	reaction
audience	drama	performance	scene
character	ending	play	scenery
classical	graphic	plot	standing ovation

41 Comparative constructions

A family

1. These are ways to express similarity or sameness.

with **like**, **similar to**, and **the same as**

> My younger brother's eyes are just **like** my father's (eyes).
> But his nose and mouth are **similar to** my mother's (nose and mouth).
> His way of talking is **the same as** mine (my way of talking).

with **alike, similar**, and **the same** (Notice the difference in pattern from the constructions above.)

> My brother's eyes and my father's are **alike**.
> His nose and mouth and my mother's are **similar**.
> His way of talking and mine are **the same**.

with **as . . . as**

> My brother is almost **as tall as** my father already.

2. These are ways to express difference.

with the negatives of the construction above.

> My brother's eyes are**n't like** my mother's.
> His nose and mouth and my father's are**n't the same**.
> He is**n't as/so tall as** my father yet.

with **different from** and **different**

> My brother's eyes are **different from** my mother's.
> His eyes and hers are **different**.

The examples above are all adjectival. Most of the same constructions can be used adverbially.

to express similarity or sameness

> My brother acts just **like** my father.
> He already weighs almost **the same as** my father (does).
> They talk a lot **alike**.
> They speak about **the same**. They speak **similarly**.
> My brother plays football **as well as** my father (does).

41 Comparative constructions

> to express difference
>
> *My younger sister doesn't act **like** my mother at all.*
> *She doesn't behave **the same as** she (does).*
> *They don't talk **alike**.*
> *They don't speak **the same**. They speak **differently**.*
> *My sister doesn't do anything **as/so well as** my mother (does). But my sister is only nine months old.*

A. Circle the correct choices in parentheses.

1. It's amazing how (different, (different from)) each other siblings can be, considering that their environment must be (the same, the same as). Although my baby sister is only nine months old, you can tell that she's going to be (like, alike) my father, and completely (different, different from) my mother. It isn't just that she and my father look (like, alike); her temperament is (the same, the same as) his. She's just as placid and easygoing as he. On the other hand, my older brother is very (similar, similar to) my mother in appearance, character, and temperament. They do a lot of things (similar, similarly). I seem to be a mixture of both parents. I look more (like, alike) my father, but my character and temperament are more (like, alike) my mother's. As they say, "Variety is the spice of life."

2. There's a pair of twins in my family, but they don't look much (like, alike). Their features are (different, differently): one's eyes and nose and mouth and chin are completely (different, different from) the other's. They wear their hair (different, differently), and their way of dressing isn't (the same, the same as) at all. One's interests aren't (the same, the same as) the other's. One of them doesn't play football nearly (as well, as well as) the other; the other doesn't draw (like, alike) the first. Probably one reason they're not very (similar, similar to) each other is that they're fraternal, not identical twins. Probably another reason they're so (different, different from) is that one is a boy, and the other is a girl.

Arthur   Mr. Brown   Mrs. Brown   Alfred   Sara   Sally

B. Use the comparative constructions below to describe the Brown family.

like *Alfred's nose is like his mother's.*
similar to _____
the same as _____
alike _____
similar _____
the same _____
as....as _____
not like _____
not the same _____
not so....as _____
different from _____
different _____
similarly _____
differently _____

Vocabulary Summary

appearance	features	mixture	twins
character	fraternal	placid	variety
easygoing	identical	siblings	way
environment	interests	temperament	

42 Adverbs of time

Old age

1. **Still** describes a state or action that extends from the past right up to the moment of speaking. Notice the various positions it takes.

In affirmative statements and questions with **be**:

> A: *Are your grandparents **still** healthy?*
> B: *Yes, they're lucky. They're also **still** in love—and they just had their golden anniversary.*
> A: *Fifty years! Wow!*

In affirmative statements and questions with other verbs:

> *Are they **still** living around here?*
> *Yes, on Maple Street. They **still** live in their first house.*

In negative statements:

> *They **still** haven't had a real fight, in all these years.*

2. **Anymore** describes a terminated state or action of the past. It is generally placed at the end of a negative sentence:

> *My grandfather retired last week; he doesn't go to the factory **anymore**.*

3. **Already** describes a state or action that is completed sooner than expected. It is generally used in affirmative statements and affirmative questions:

> *Grandfather worked at the factory for 55 years, but he says he's "**already**" retired. On his first day home, Grandmother forgot he'd retired. At two o'clock, she said, "Are you **already** home?"*

Already may also go at the end of the sentence:

> *He's retired "**already**."*
> *"Are you home **already**?"*

4. **Yet** describes a state or action that is later than expected. It is usually placed at the end of questions and negative statements:

> *Is your grandmother used to having your grandfather home **yet**?*
> *I don't think she's used to it **yet**. She still wakes him up at 5:30.*

Adverbs of time 42

149

A. Rewrite the following conversations with older people. Add **still, anymore, already,** or **yet** to each underlined part. In some cases, there are two possible answers.

1. **Pete:** Are you working?
   Henry: I don't work full-time, but I'm working part-time.
   Pete: *Are you still working?*
   Henry: _____

2. **Mr. Eastman:** How's your health?
   Mr. Lewis: Pretty good. I can't believe I'm 75 years old. Of course I can't do a lot of things I used to do. I don't drive much at night, and I'm not the athlete I used to be. But I have all my own teeth, and my eyesight's good. I have all my faculties. No, I'm not ready to give up.
   Mr. Eastman: _____
   Mr. Lewis: _____

3. **Manuel:** Are you retired? You look so young!
   George: Well, thank you. I like to think that I haven't started to show my age.
   Manuel: You're lucky. Look at me: 45 years old and I look ten years older. I've got false teeth!
   George: You look pretty youthful to me, young man, but then I've got thirty years on you. Everybody looks young to me!
   Manuel: _____
   George: _____
   Manuel: _____
   George: _____

42 Adverbs of time

4. **Erik:** You say your husband is 86? And he hasn't retired?
   Mrs. Potter: That's right. As far as I can see, he hasn't slowed down much at all.
   Erik: That's amazing. I'm 50, I'm looking forward to retirement, and I've slowed up a lot.
   Erik: _____
   Mrs. Potter: _____
   _____
   Erik: _____
   _____

5. **The Judge:** How do you feel about getting older?
   The Teacher: Oh, there are things you can't do, but there are compensations. Have you ever read Tennyson's "Ulysses"?
   The Judge: I've heard of it, but I haven't read it.
   The Teacher: Well, in it Ulysses knows he's coming to the end of his life, but he isn't ready to die. He hopes he can go sailing with his men one more time. He says that old age has "its honor and its toil." He's "strong in will to strive, to seek, to find, and not to yield."
   The Judge: That's beautiful. I feel that way now, and I hope I do when I reach the end of my life.
   The Judge: _____
   The Teacher: _____
   _____
   The Judge: _____
   The Teacher: _____
   _____
   _____
   _____
   _____
   The Judge: _____
   _____

B. Complete the paragraphs about Ulysses with **still, anymore, already,** and **yet**.

There is a major difference between the story of Ulysses as told by Homer and Tennyson's version of it 2,700 years later. According to Homer, all of the other heros of the Trojan War went back home after the war, but Ulysses wasn't allowed

Adverbs of time

Ulysses

by the gods to go home _____. He _____ had to wander for years. During this time, his wife and son thought he was dead, but the goddess Athena appeared to his son and said that Ulysses was _____ alive. His son then searched for Ulysses, found him, and returned home with him. After he was reunited with his family, Ulysses didn't wander _____; he had _____ been away for many years and was content to stay.

According to Tennyson, however, Ulysses _____ wanted to make one last voyage with his sailors. He wasn't ready to stop having adventures _____ even though he wasn't young _____. He _____ wanted to see places in the world that he hadn't _____ seen. In the illustration, we see Ulysses about to leave on his last voyage. His ship is _____ prepared to sail, and Ulysess is saying goodbye to his faithful dog. They probably know that they won't see each other _____ after this fairwell.

Vocabulary Summary

anniversary	get old	part-time	slow up
compensation	give up	retire	strive
eyesight	golden anniversary	retirement	toil
faculties	health	seek	will (desire)
false teeth	honor	show (one's) age	yield
full-time	look forward to	slow down	youthful

43 Adverbs of degree

Weights and measures

1. **Very** means **extremely**. It precedes the adjective or adverb it modifies:

   *This box of canned goods is **very** heavy. It must weigh 50 pounds. I'm not sure I can lift it.*

   Other adverbs of degree that have the same pattern as **very** include these:

less extreme	more extreme
pretty*	awfully*
quite	terribly
rather	extremely
somewhat	really

   *informal

2. **Too** means **excessively**. It also precedes the adjective or adverb it modifies. An infinitive phrase may follow the adjective or adverb:

   *This box of books is **too** heavy. It must weigh a ton. I can't lift it. It's **too** heavy (for me) **to lift**.*

3. **Enough** means **sufficiently**. It follows the adjective or adverb it modifies. (When **enough** modifies a noun, it may precede or follow: *I don't have **enough** time/time **enough** to talk right now*.) An infinitive phrase may follow **enough**:

   *This box of pillows is light **enough**. It must weigh only a few pounds. I can lift it easily. It's light **enough** (for me) **to lift**.*

A. Fill in each blank with an adverb of degree (such as **very**, **too**, or **enough**). (Remember that other words such as **quite** can take the place of **very**.)

1. Tom is 6'7". He's _very_ tall. Margie is 4'10". She's _____ short. Margie doesn't want to go out with Tom. She thinks she isn't tall _____ for him, and he's _____ tall for her.

2. Slim is 5'10" and weighs 105 lbs. He thinks he's _____ thin, so he's going on a special diet to gain some weight. He doesn't think he's heavy _____ for his height.

153   **Adverbs of degree**   *43*

3. That measuring spoon isn't big _____. No, don't use a measuring cup, either. That would be _____ big. You need a tablespoon. That would be exactly big _____.

4. I may need help lifting this. It's _____ heavy...Ooof!...On second thought, I definitely need help. It's _____ heavy. It must weigh 150 pounds. I'm not strong _____ to lift it by myself.

5. You won't be able to put 8 1/2 X 11" paper into your typewriter the long way. The carriage isn't wide _____ , only 10 1/2". You'll have to use a typewriter with a wide _____ carriage or else put the paper in the other way.

Some Weights and Measures

weight
1 pound (lb.) = 453.59 grams
16 ounces (oz.) = 1 lb.
2,000 lbs. = 1 ton

length
1 inch (") = 2.54 centimeters
12" = 1 foot (')
3' = 1 yard (yd.)
1 yd. = .9 meters
5,280' (1,760 yds.) = 1 mile (mi.)
1 mi. = 1.6 kilometers

capacity
1 teaspoon (t./tsp.) = 5 milliliters
3 t. = 1 tablespoon (T./tbsp.)
4 T. = ¼ cup (2 oz.)
8 oz. = 1 cup

2 cups = 1 pint
2 pints = 1 quart
4 quarts = 1 gallon
1 gallon = 3.8 liters

---

6. You say you're getting 30 miles to a gallon with your new car? That's really _____ good. Mine doesn't do _____ well. I get only about 15 miles to a gallon in city driving -- not good _____ .

7. I don't think a mile is two and a half kilometers. That sounds like _____ many. 1.6? That sounds close _____ .

8. Don't try to pour the milk into that glass. You've got three cups of milk there, and the glass will only hold two. It's _____ small.

9. You want to walk to the train station? Are you kidding? It's _____ far to walk, and your bags are _____ heavy to carry. You can't be _____ serious about walking!

10. Aren't there four pints in a quart? No? _____ many? Oh, two pints in a quart, and four quarts in a gallon. I guess my memory for measurements isn't _____ good.

43 Adverbs of degree   154

B: Complete these sentences.

The hat is big.
It's too ___*big*___ for Tim,
but ___*big enough*___ for Tom.

1. The shirt is very small.
   It's too _____ for Tom,
   but big _____ for Tim.

2. The pants are quite large.
   They're _____ for Tom,
   but _____ for Tim.

3. The belt is very long.
   It's _____ for Tim,
   but _____ for Tom.

4. The shoes are small.
   They're _____ small for Tom,
   but _____ for Tim.

5. Tom's shorts are tight; in fact,
   they're _____ for him.

6. Tim's shorts are loose, but
   they're _____ for Tom.

44 Word order of adverbials

Museums

Adverbials of place, manner, frequency, and time may be single words such as **here**, expressions such as **every now and then**, or phrases such as **at ten o'clock**.

The usual order of adverbials is: **place, manner, frequency, time**.

They usually take the following positions in sentences:

1. Adverbials of **place** go after the verb and its object, if there is one.

    *The main entrance to the Metropolitan **is on Fifth Avenue**.*

2. Adverbials of **manner** go after the verb and its object, if any.

    *We **got to** the Prado **by taxi**.*

    Adverbs ending in **-ly** may also go before the main verb and after the first auxiliary, if there is one.

    *Visitors to Bermuda **can quickly learn** about its history at the Bermuda Historical Museum in Hamilton. You **should certainly have visited** it.*

3. Adverbials of **frequency** regularly take these positions:

    All single-word adverbials of frequency go after forms of **be**.

    *I for one **am usually** exhausted after about twenty minutes in any museum.*

    Always, never, seldom, usually, and **ever** (which is used in questions and in negative statements) go before other verbs and after the first auxiliary, if there is one.

    ***Have** you **ever seen** the mosaics at Istanbul's Mosque of Sultan Ahmet?*

    Other single-word adverbials of frequency may go either before the verb (except forms of **be**) or after the verb and its object.

    *Trude **frequently visits** the Rijksmuseum in Amsterdam.*
    *Trude **visits** the Rijksmuseum in Amsterdam **frequently**.*

    Expressions and phrases go after the verb and its object, if there is one.

    *There's a new exhibit in the Morgan Gallery **at least once a month**.*

44 Word order of adverbials 156

> 4. Adverbials of **time** usually go after the verb and its object, if there is one.
>
> *Carlos **wants** to see the pre-Inca artifacts at the Tiwanaku Museum in La Paz **this weekend**.*
>
> **Immediately, now, recently,** and **soon** may also go before the main verb.
>
> *Hideaki **recently went** to the Tokyo National Museum for the first time.*

A. Mark each of these words, expressions, and phrases as adverbials of **Place**, **Manner**, **Frequency**, or **Time**.

_M_	1.	with no noticeable accent
___	2.	during a night of mystery
___	3.	every once in a while
___	4.	elegantly
___	5.	hardly ever
___	6.	past the display of rare butterflies
___	7.	immediately, if not sooner
___	8.	across the marble-tiled floor
___	9.	daily
___	10.	at eight

B. Rewrite each sentence, adding the adverbial in parentheses. When lines are marked **a** and **b**, write the sentence with the adverbial in two different positions.

I'll meet you. (at the museum gift shop)
I'll meet you at the museum gift shop.

1. You'll find the antique furniture. (on the third floor)
   _____

2. The new anthropology curator has worked to improve the collection. (hard)
   _____
   _____

3. Hilda doesn't like modern sculpture, so she ignores that exhibit. (happily)
   a. _____
   _____

Word order of adverbials   44

   b. _____

4. Turner's vivid paintings are on display at London's Tate. (always)
   _____

5. Peggy lives in Rochester, but for some reason she's visited Eastman House. (never)
   _____

6. Since the big robbery, someone checks the museum's security system. (regularly)
   a. _____

   b. _____

7. Shouldn't somebody dust off these fossils? (once a year or so)
   _____

8. I'd like to see the Etruscan art at the Villa Giulia. (someday)
   _____

9. The Huntington will be announcing a major acquisition. (soon)
   a. _____

   b. _____

C. Write complete sentences, putting the adverbials in parentheses in the correct order. Some are correct as they are.

1. When we went (last year, to Cairo), we saw the superb Tutankhamen collection at the Egyptian Museum.
   _____

2. The dinosaur skeleton was (this morning, right here). Where could it be?
   _____

44 Word order of adverbials 158

3. People always seem to talk (in hushed voices, in museums).

4. A woman just ran (with a priceless Ming vase, out the front door)!

5. Their collection of ancient Roman coins has been increased (during the last year, dramatically) by anonymous gifts.

6. I swear I saw that Greek statue wink at me (surreptitiously, a second ago).

7. The painting that was (always, on that wall) was recently defaced by vandals.

8. Mireille goes (by the Louvre, every morning) on her way to work at the perfume factory.

D. In this conversation between two potential thieves, some of the adverbials are in the wrong position. Rewrite the conversation with all the adverbials correctly placed.

Lefty: Have you noticed ever the diamond they on display have at the museum?
Gill: Noticed! I have sure! I at least once a week stop in with awe to gaze at it.
Lefty: Well, ever have you thought about stealing it?
Gill: Get serious. I just last night dreamed about it. But always there's in front of it a security guard.
Lefty: There's one at night never. I know because I've there been for the last week hiding after the museum closes. On duty there's all night for the whole museum only one guard. Past the diamond he once every hour walks, but that's it!
Gill: So are you tonight doing anything?
Lefty: *Have you*
Gill:

159 Word order of adverbials 44

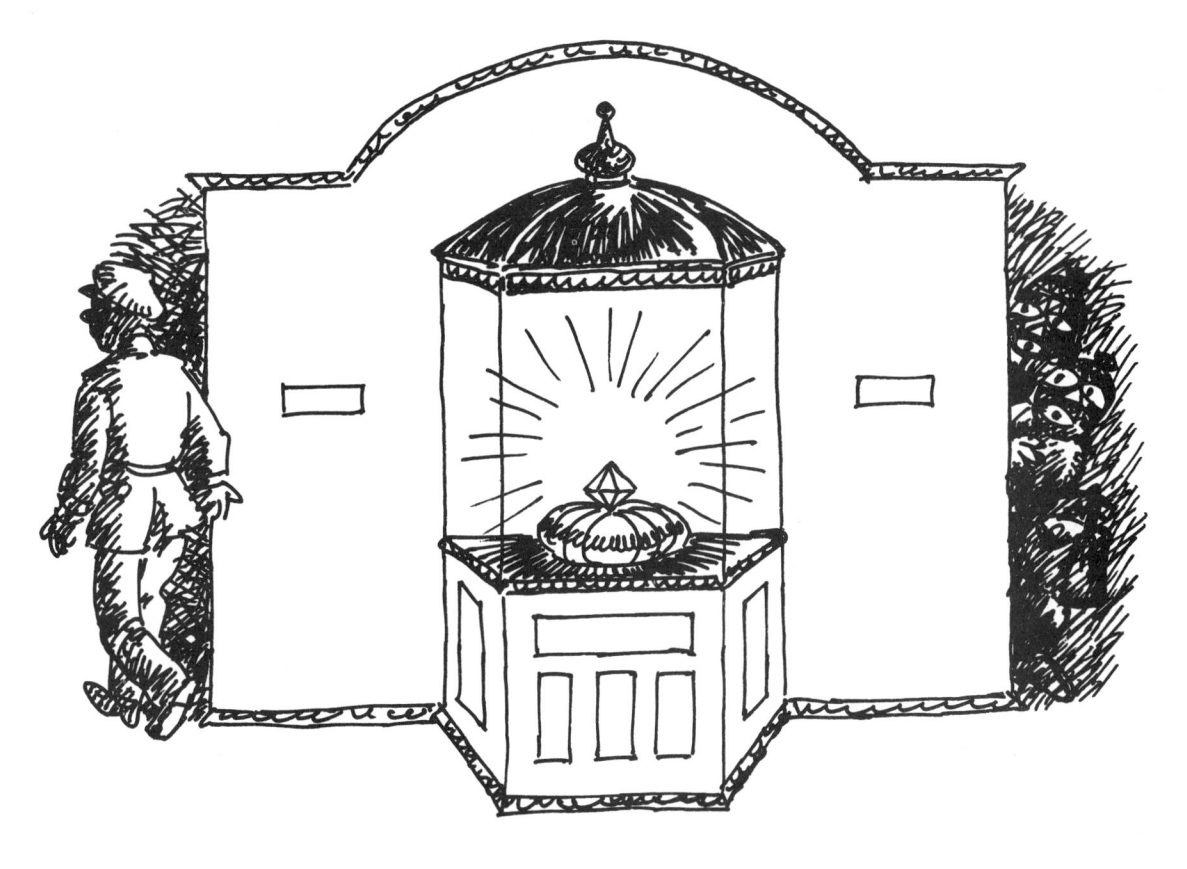

Lefty: _____

Gill: _____
_____

Lefty: _____
_____
_____
_____

Gill: _____

Vocabulary Summary

acquisition	deface	historical	rare
ancient	diamond	history	robbery
anonymous	dinosaur	marble	sculpture
anthropology	display	modern	security system
antique	entrance	mosaic	skeleton
art	exhibit	mosque	statue
artifact	fossil	museum	thief, thieves
butterfly	gallery	painting	vandal
collection	gift shop	pre-Inca	vase
curator	guard	priceless	

45 Miscellaneous prepositions

Tips for householders

These are some uses of prepositions:

1. method (transportation) — **by, on**

    *If your supermarket isn't too far away, go **on foot** rather than **by car, bus, or cab**. You'll not only save money but get some exercise.*

2. manner — **in, like, with**

    *Buy **in large lots** when possible.*
    *Grate onions quickly **like this**: score from the top and then slice.*
    *Routine household tasks can be done **with ease** if you have the right materials.*

3. means (agent or instrument) — **by, with**

    *Never try to loosen a stubborn lid **by hitting the jar against the floor**.*
    *Don't try to open it **with a hammer** either.*

Notice that all of the above prepositional phrases answer the question "How...?"

4. purpose — **for**

    *You can buy a machine **for grinding coffee beans**, but would it be worth it?*

5. association — **of**

    *One of the secrets **of efficiency** around the house is to make lists **of things to be done** and cross them off as you accomplish them.*

6. measure — **by, of**

    *There's no point in buying fruits and vegetables **by the bushel** if you can't use them up before they spoil.*
    *A pinch **of sugar** in almost any dish will bring out the flavor.*

7. in the capacity of — **as**

    *You can use a plastic milk carton **as a planter**.*

8. accompaniment — **with**

    *If you tend to be an impulse buyer, go shopping **with someone who's more levelheaded**.*

Miscellaneous prepositions — 45

Label text:

This paste, created for you by grinding the all-natural pits of ripe tropical fruit with millstones carved from The Sacred Himalayas and then blending in the powdered shells of the purple sea urchin of Hecate Strait, B.C., may be used

- for cleaning your teeth and nails
- for the removal of excess body hair
- as an antacid, natural cure for all cramps, and heartburn.
- for the effortless cleansing of brass and other hard-to-clean materials

DREAM CREME deluxe

A miracle of science in a jar

Instructions:
When used as a curative, take a spoonful of creme with a glass of milk or vodka.

When used for personal beautification, blend with equal parts of butter and apply by the handful to the skin.

When used as a toothpaste, apply with a toothbrush like any paste in small quantities.

When used as a cleanser or spot remover on any surface of wood, cloth, plastic, or metal, rub in a fingerful of creme at a time, dry, and carefully scrape clean.

A. Underline all the prepositions on this label. Then list below one prepositional phrase of --

Manner: _____

Means: _____

Purpose: _____

Association: _____

Measure: _____

Capacity: _____

Accompaniment: _____

45 Miscellaneous prepositions

B. Fill in each blank with a preposition.

1. To clean tarnished silver, put a piece _____ aluminum foil in a glass dish. Add the silver, and cover it _____ a quart _____ hot water mixed _____ four tablespoons _____ baking soda. The reaction between the mixture and the foil acts _____ an agent _____ removing the tarnish.

2. To loosen a stuck window _____ ease, put a block _____ wood against the sash at various places. Tap the block _____ a hammer.

3. You can save money _____ buying food _____ large amounts, such as cases _____ canned goods, or vegetables _____ the bushel.

4. Most stains can be removed from carpets _____ cleaning them _____ club soda or _____ a mixture _____ equal parts _____ white vinegar and water.

5. Buy local produce when possible, rather than that brought in _____ truck or _____ freight. It will taste better and be fresher and more nutritious.

6. Leave a dish _____ vinegar or ammonia in the room overnight to get rid of bad, stale odors. Or make the whole place smell _____ fresh baked goods _____ shaking some powdered cloves in a pan _____ water and heating it on the stove.

7. Keep baking soda on hand _____ an extinguisher _____ small emergency kitchen fires. Never use water _____ putting out electric, oil, or grease fires.

45 Miscellaneous prepositions

8. You can make your own versions _____ more expensive commercial household cleaners _____ little expense _____ using common materials found around the house. For example, you can polish copper and brass _____ a paste mixture _____ hot vinegar and salt.

9. If you feel overwhelmed _____ what seems like too big a household task, do it _____ small steps, _____ a series _____ separate tasks.

10. Here are some general tips _____ saving money on food:

    * Plan meals _____ the week.

    * Buy _____ the largest practical quantities.

    * Eat more of what you pay for. For example, cook such parts as cauliflower leaves and stems and serve them _____ extra vegetables.

    * Use leftovers _____ different combinations _____ "new" dishes. _____ these hints, you'll be saving money _____ an expert _____ no time!

Vocabulary Summary

accomplish	efficiency	keep house	score
aluminum foil	extinguisher	leftovers	silver
ammonia	flavor	lid	slice
baked goods	go shopping	loosen	spoil
baking soda	grate	lot (amount)	stain
brass	grease	nutritious	stale
bushel	grind	odor	stuck
canned goods	hammer	oil	supermarket
carton	(on) hand	pinch	tarnish
case	hint	practical	task
cauliflower	household	produce (n.)	tip (pointer)
cloves	householder	quantity	use up
club soda	impulse	routine	vinegar
copper	jar	sash	

46 Prepositions in fixed phrases
Mr. Crabbe's opinions

1. Two words or more may act as a single prepositional unit:

according to	because of	in addition to
ahead of	by means of	in case of
as a result of	contrary to	in favor of
as well as	except for	in spite of
at/in (the) back of	for the sake of	on account of

   *I'm not going to agree with you just **for the sake of** being agreeable.*

2. Some verbs are normally followed by specific prepositions:

(dis)agree on (something)	belong to	interfere with
(dis)agree with (someone)	(not) care for	object to
approve of	complain about	succeed in
argue with	differ from	vote for
believe in	insist on/upon	watch out for

   *I **insist upon** being heard.*

3. Some specific prepositions are normally used with certain verbs in this pattern:

   verb + object + **preposition** + object

   blame someone **for** something
   blame something **on** someone
   congratulate someone **for/on** something
   excuse someone **for** something
   prefer one person or thing **to** another
   remind someone **of** something

   *Well, excuse me **for** living!*

4. Some adjectives and participles are normally followed by specific prepositions:

aware of	different from	interested in
certain of	disgusted by/with	opposed to
content with	fit for	positive of
critical of	guilty of	(dis)satisfied with
deficient in	happy about/with	surprised at/by

   *I have an open mind. I'm not **opposed to** anyone except those who don't agree with me.*

Prepositions in fixed phrases 46

Mr. Crabbe is opinionated, irascible, and cantankerous. Above all, he likes writing letters to people and institutions he disagrees with or has a complaint about. Mr. Crabbe knows that his attitude is often rude and doesn't win him any friends, but he can't seem to stop. These are excerpts from some of Mr. Crabbe's recent letters. Fill in the missing prepositions. Try not to look back at the lists in the introduction.

Of course your opinions are different *from* mine. That's because yours are wrong and misguided.

1. I insist _____ receiving a refund for the Happy cereal I bought, which isn't fit _____ even a dog to eat.

2. I would like to argue this issue _____ you in person, but because _____ my age, I am unable to travel. Perhaps a representative of your company would be interested _____ traveling here to discuss the problem with me.

3. Contrary _____ your opinion, according _____ every authority I have consulted, you are dead wrong. In addition _____ disagreeing _____ you, they object strongly _____ your openly airing your mistaken ideas.

4. I was absolutely disgusted _____ your six o'clock news last night. You are surely deficient _____ common sense, putting such trash on TV. As a result _____ my displeasure, I am switching to Channel 30 from now on. (I always preferred their news _____ yours anyway.) You have succeeded _____ alienating this viewer, and I hope you receive hundreds of letters from others complaining _____ your irresponsible journalism.

46 Prepositions in fixed phrases

5. It's you politicians who are to blame _____ everything that's wrong with this country. It's beyond me how any sensible person could have voted ____ you or be in favor _____ your policies. I've noticed that even people who belong _____ your party and formerly believed _____ what you were doing are now surprised _____ and dissatisfied _____ your actions. In spite _____ the fact that politicians have to compromise, which I am well aware _____, it seems clear that everything you are doing now is for the sake _____ expediency. Personally I am opposed _____ everything you apparently approve _____.

6. I am positive _____ my opinion as well _____ critical _____ yours. I can excuse you _____ having mistaken opinions (I have occasionally been guilty _____ that myself, but not often), but not _____ being so certain _____ your own rectitude.

7. I am writing to you once again to say that I am not happy _____ conditions at your supermarket. Far be it from me to interfere _____ how you run your business, but I don't understand how you can be content _____ it as it is. It reminds me _____ a zoo. On account _____ the number of shoppers with small children, one has to constantly watch out _____ flying cartons of canned goods and runaway shopping carts. The aisles are too narrow, particularly in the back _____ the store. One can get through them only by means _____ careful maneuvering. I shudder to think of what would happen in case _____ a fire.

I congratulate you _____ having fired that check-out clerk at the second register, but the new one is no improvement. What happened to me there yesterday, I blame _____ him entirely: someone actually cut ahead ____ me in line, and he did nothing about it!

Unless conditions improve, I will be forced to take my business elsewhere.

Adjective clauses   47

The dating game

> A clause has a subject and a verb and is part of a sentence. Noun, adverb, and adjective (relative) clauses are all dependent clauses; they cannot stand alone as sentences.
>
> Adjective clauses follow and modify nouns and pronouns. They are introduced by relative pronouns: **who, whom, whose, which,** and **that**.
>
> **Who** refers to people. It is the subject of the clause. **That** can replace **who**.
>
> > *I want to meet someone. + **He's tall and blonde.**=*
> > *I want to meet someone **who's tall and blonde**.*
> > *I want to meet someone **that's tall and blonde**.*
>
> **Whom** is the object form of **who**. **That** can replace **whom**. As objects, both can be omitted from the clause.
>
> > *He'd be like no one. + **I've never met him.** =*
> > *He'd be like no one **whom I've ever met**.*
> > *He'd be like no one **that I've ever met**.*
> > *He'd be like no one **I've ever met**.*
>
> **Whose** is possessive.
>
> > *But he'd be someone. + **I'd recognize his face instantly.**=*
> > *But he'd be someone **whose face I'd recognize instantly**.*
>
> **Which** refers to things. It is used when the clause is set off by commas.
>
> > *I'd know his face anywhere. + **I've seen it in my dreams.**=*
> > *I'd know his face, **which I've seen in my dreams**, anywhere.*

Combine the pairs of sentences into sentences with adjective clauses. Use commas as indicated, and write two or three sentences wherever possible.

1. Would you like to go to the prom with my sister? Her date got sick. (Use a comma.)

   _____

   _____

47 Adjective clauses   168

2. Isn't she the one? She's about six feet tall.

   a. _____
      _____

   b. _____
      _____

3. She's at least six inches taller than I am. That could make dancing difficult. (Use a comma.)
   _____
   _____

4. I think I'll go with Luisa. She's closer to my height. (Use a comma.)
   _____
   _____

5. Personally, I like women. They're taller than I am.

   a. _____
      _____

   b. _____
      _____

6. Chantal is taller than my sister. I went out with her for a year. (Use two commas.)
   _____
   _____

7. I have a friend. I'd like you to meet him.

   a. _____
      _____

   b. _____
      _____

   c. _____
      _____

8. He's a man. He's not terribly good-looking, but he has a wonderful personality.

   a. _____
      _____

   b. _____
      _____

9. He's someone. I'm sure you'll enjoy meeting him.

   a. _____
      _____

   b. _____
      _____

Adjective clauses 47

169

   c. _____

10. He has a brother, but I'm going out with him. He's a real hunk.

   a. _____

   b. _____

11. What do you think about women? They go out with younger men.

   a. _____

   b. _____

12. I think the same as you do about men. They go out with younger women.

   a. _____

   b. _____

13. I have an uncle. His girlfriend is eighteen years younger than he is.

   _____

14. My cousin is really happy. Her boyfriend is nine years younger than she is. (Use two commas.)

   _____

15. People should be able to go out with anyone, regardless of age. They like them.

   a. _____

   b. _____

   c. _____

48 Adverb clauses of time

Autobiography

Some of the conjunctions that introduce adverb clauses of time are **when, while, since, until, before,** and **after**. Like adjective clauses, adverb clauses are dependent (see lesson 47).

1. **When** means "**at** the time that . . ."

   When I was born, my parents were living near Kalamazoo.

2. **While** means "**during** the time that . . ."

   My father was sick and couldn't work for two years. My mother worked in a canning factory while he was unemployed.

3. **Since** means "**starting from** the time that . . ."

   I haven't seen my older brother since he left home at 16.

4. **Until** means "**up to** the time that . . ."

   We lived near Kalamazoo until my younger brother was born.

5. **Before** and **after** refer to a sequence of time.

   Before I was 17, I was married and expecting a baby.
   My husband and I moved to Chillicothe after our daughter was born.

When the adverb clause is at the beginning of the sentence, it is usually followed by a comma. There is usually no comma when the clause is at the end of the sentence.

Use the present tense for future time in clauses with **when, while, until, before,** and **after.**

   When my husband finishes his apprenticeship, he'll be a skilled cabinetmaker.

Using the autobiographical information below, complete the sentences with adverb clauses of time. Use **when, while, since, until, before,** and **after**. Be sure each clause has a subject and a verb. Use a comma where it is indicated.

When David Putnam was born, _____ ,
his parents were living in Hartford, Connecticut.

Autobiography of David Putnam 1940

Born May 28, 1940; parents living in Hartford, Connecticut
5/41 - family moved to Windsor, Vermont; parents still there
sister born August 4, 1942
father in Navy 9/43 - end of war
mother worked at Upson factory '43-'46
father began working there '45
worked part-time at drugstore '56-'58
graduated from Windsor High 6/58
Colby College '58-'62
met Jean at Colby '60
married Jean 6/24/63
also '63 -- bought house in New London, began work at shipyard
daughter, Vicki, born 7/9/65
son, Chuck, born 8/11/67
promoted to superintendent '70
moved to Waterford '72

Vocabulary Summary

apprenticeship	factory	move (change residence)	(be) promoted
(be) born	graduate (from)	Navy	superintendent
cabinetmaker	leave home	parents	unemployed
(be) expecting (a baby)	(be) married	part-time	war
	marry		

48 Adverb clauses of time 172

1. He was born on May 28, 1940, _____.

2. His parents lived in Hartford _____
   _____.

3. _____,
   his parents were living in Windsor, Vermont.

4. _____,
   his sister was born, on August 4, 1942.

5. His parents have lived in Windsor, Vermont, _____
   _____.

6. They moved to Windsor a year _____,
   and a year _____.

7. From September '43 _____,
   his father was in the Navy.

8. His mother worked at the Upson factory _____
   _____.

9. His mother kept working at Upson for a year _____
   _____.

10. _____,
    he worked part-time at a drug store.

11. _____,
    he went to Colby College.

12. He met Jean _____
    _____.

13. A year _____,
    he graduated from Colby.

14. He's been working at the shipyard ever _____
    _____.

15. Their daughter was born a little more than two years _____
    _____.

16. _____,
    he was promoted to superintendent.

17. They lived in New London for nine years _____
    _____.

49 Adverb clauses of reason
Natural wonders

1. Adverb clauses of reason may be introduced by **because** or **since**:

   Because/Since *earthquakes disturbed its flow, the geyser called Old Faithful no longer erupts regularly.*

   The idea of the clause can often be reduced to a prepositional phrase with **because of**, with changes in wording:

   Because of *earthquakes, the geyser called Old Faithful no longer erupts regularly.*

2. Adverb clauses of concession may be introduced by **although** or **though**:

   *People still flock to see Old Faithful **although/though** it fails to erupt regularly.*

   The idea of the clause can often be reduced to a prepositional phrase with **in spite of** or **despite**, with changes in wording:

   *People still flock to see Old Faithful **in spite of/despite** its failure to erupt regularly.*

   Notice that when the clause or phrase begins the sentence, a comma usually follows it. When it ends the sentence, there is usually no comma before it.

A. Combine each pair of sentences with **because/since** or **although/though**.

The heating system in Iceland (9) is cheap. The country has a large number of hot springs.

The heating system in Iceland is cheap because the country has a large number of hot springs.

1. Niagara Falls (7) is relatively small. It's still very impressive, especially from the Canadian side.

   _____

   _____

2. Mount St. Helens (5) hasn't erupted violently again. It's been making ominous sounds and spewing some lava.

   _____

   _____

Natural Wonders

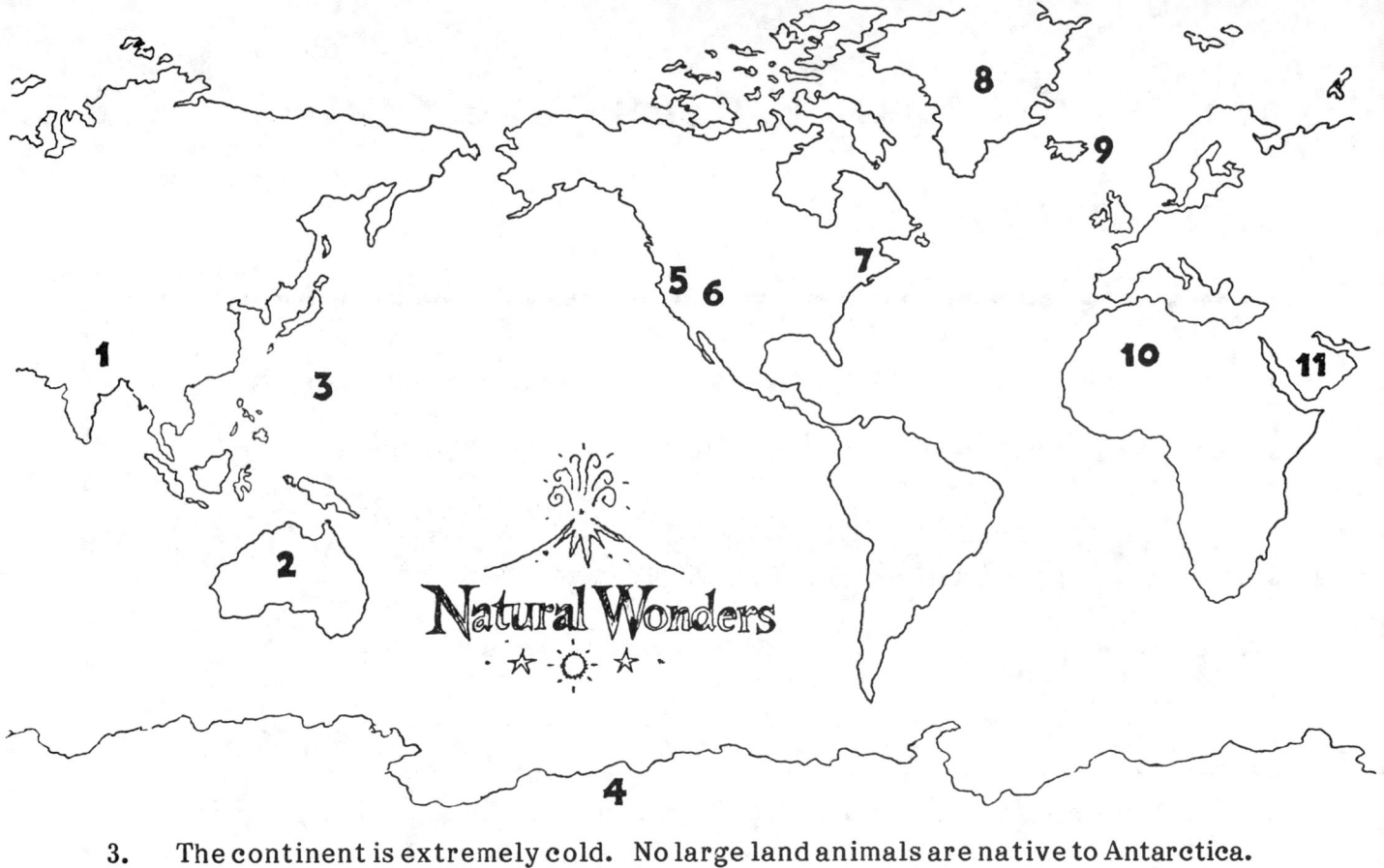

3. The continent is extremely cold. No large land animals are native to Antarctica.

4. Earthquakes are awesomely able to destroy. Fewer people are killed by earthquakes themselves than by the following tidal waves.

5. Many mountaineering groups use the 1850 figure of 29,002 feet for Mount Everest (1). A figure of 29,028 feet was established in 1954 by the Indian government.

6. Many attempt to climb Mount Everest (1), but few reach its peak. Its altitude and dangers are great.

7. It's extremely deep. No one has ever reached the bottom of the Pacific Ocean's Mariana Trench (3), at 38,635 feet.

8. The world's largest island is Greenland (8) (840,000 square miles), not Australia (2) (2,939,975 square miles). Australia's status is as a continent.

49 Adverb clauses of reason and concession

9. The Sahara (10) is the largest tropical and climatic desert in the world. The Rub al-Khali (11) is the world's largest continuous sand area.
_____
_____

B. Rewrite each sentence in exercise A with a prepositional phrase in place of the clause. Use the nouns or gerunds in parentheses, and make all other necessary changes. Remember possessive forms where necessary.

(number) *The heating system in Iceland is cheap because of the country's large number of hot springs.*

1. (size) _____

2. (making, spewing) _____

3. (cold) _____

4. (ability) _____

5. (figure) _____

6. (altitude, dangers) _____

7. (depth) _____

8. (status) _____

9. (being) _____

Vocabulary Summary

altitude	flow	Mount Everest	Sahara
climatic	geyser	Mount St. Helens	sand
desert	hot springs	mountaineering	spew
earthquake	impressive	Niagara Falls	springs
erupt	lava	peak	tidal wave
flock (v.)	Mariana Trench	Rub al-Khali	tropical

50 Conditional clauses: real

Etiquette

There are three main types of sentence with **if** clauses and real conditional clauses.

	the verb in the **if clause**	the verb in the **main clause**
1	present tense or modal + simple form *If I **can't be** there,*	simple future or modal + simple form *I**'ll let** you know in advance.*
2	present or modal *If you're **planning** to bring a friend,*	a request form *you **should tell** your host or hostess.*
3	present or modal *If I **stay** overnight at someone's house,*	present or modal *I always **take** a gift.*

Type 1 expresses a situation that can or will happen under the conditions in the **if** clause. It is sometimes called "future possible."

Type 2 expresses a request, a suggestion, or an obligation under the conditions in the **if** clause.

Type 3 expresses a situation that generally happens under the conditions in the **if** clause. **If** has the meaning of **whenever**.

The main clause can also precede the **if** clause, usually with no comma.

I'll let you know in advance if I can't be there.

50 Conditional clauses: real

A. Write the sentences with the appropriate forms of the verbs in parentheses.

If you'____ sure of which fork to use, _____ what your host or hostess does. (not be, watch)

If you're not sure of which fork to use, watch what your host or hostess does.

1. You _____ a small gift, such as flowers or a bottle of wine, if you'_____ to someone's house for dinner. (should take, be invited)

2. It'_____ only polite to tell your hostess or host if you'_____ to accept an invitation. (be, not be able)

3. If you _____ something stuck in your throat at dinner, _____ yourself and _____ the table. (get, excuse, leave)

4. It's impolite to ask who other guests will be or say, "I _____ if X _____ there." (not go, be)

5. If people _____ dinner together in a restaurant, it'_____ not unusual for each to pay for his or her own meal, or "go Dutch." (have, be)

6. However, if one person _____ on paying for all, another _____ to pay the tip. (insist, can offer)

7. "_____ you _____ offended if I'_____ to join you tonight?" is one rather formal way of declining an invitation. (be, not be able)

8. O.K., I promise that if anyone _____ the subject of politics at dinner, I _____ anything. (bring up, not say)

50 Conditional clauses: real

9. _____ you also _____ quiet if they _____ religion, another subject that shouldn't be discussed at the table? (keep, mention)

10. What _____ I _____ if Selma and Jim _____ us something I hate, like tripe or rhubarb? (should do, serve)

11. If you' _____ a food you don't like, just _____ it; _____ a point of talking about it. (be served, leave, not make)

12. How _____ you _____ me know if you _____ it's time to go home? (let, think)

13. If you _____ me give you a meaningful look, I _____ my throat and say, "Well....," the way people always do when they're about to leave. (not see, clear)

14. If I' _____ a good time, maybe I _____ to leave. What _____ you _____ then? (have, not want, do)

B. Rewrite your answers to the sentences from Exercise A, changing the order of the **if** and main clauses.

If you're not sure of which fork to use, watch what your host or hostess does.

Watch what your host or hostess does if you're not sure of which fork to use.

Conditional clauses: real 50

1. _____
2. _____
3. _____
4. _____
5. _____
6. _____
7. _____
8. _____
9. _____
10. _____
11. _____
12. _____
13. _____
14. _____

Vocabulary Summary

accept	go Dutch	let (someone) know	politics
(in) advance	guest	make a point of	religion
decline	have a good time	mind (v.)	serve
etiquette	host	offended	tip
excuse oneself	hostess	overnight	
formal	impolite	permission	
gift	invitation	polite	

51 Conditional clauses: unreal

Card and board games

There are two main types of sentence with **if** clauses and unreal (hypothetical or contrary-to-fact) conditions.

	the verb in the **if clause**	the verb in the **main clause**
1	present tense or future time past tense or **could** or **should** + simple form *If I **were*** a gambler (I'm not),* ***Were** is the form of **be** used for all persons.	**would, could,** or **might** + simple form *I'**d bet** on this bridge hand.*
2	past time past perfect or **could have** + past participle *If I **could have gotten** one more heart (I couldn't),*	**would, could,** or **might have** + past participle *I **could have won** the trick.*

The main clause can also precede the **if** clause, usually with no comma.

I'd bet on this bridge hand if I were a gambler.

A. Change each sentence to one with an **if** clause and an unreal condition. Keep the ideas in the same order. If a clause is affirmative, make it negative, and vice versa.

I'm going to bet on this bridge hand because I'm a gambler.

<u>I wouldn't bet on this bridge hand if I weren't a gambler.</u>

51 Conditional clauses: unreal

Because I couldn't get one more heart, I couldn't win the trick.
If I could have gotten one more heart, I could have won the trick.

1. Because spades aren't trump, I don't have a good hand.

2. I didn't do better because I didn't have clubs or diamonds.

3. I'm not glad to play hearts because you're not teaching me how.

4. You won the poker game because you cheated.

5. Because some of the tiles are missing, we can't play Scrabble.

6. Because I don't have more friends, I have to play solitaire.

7. We can't play pinochle because we can't find one more person.

8. You won at black jack because I wasn't the dealer.

9. We didn't play backgammon because I sold my set.

10. Because it seems so childish, I won't enjoy fish.

11. Because you didn't pay attention, we lost that trick.

51 Conditional clauses: unreal 182

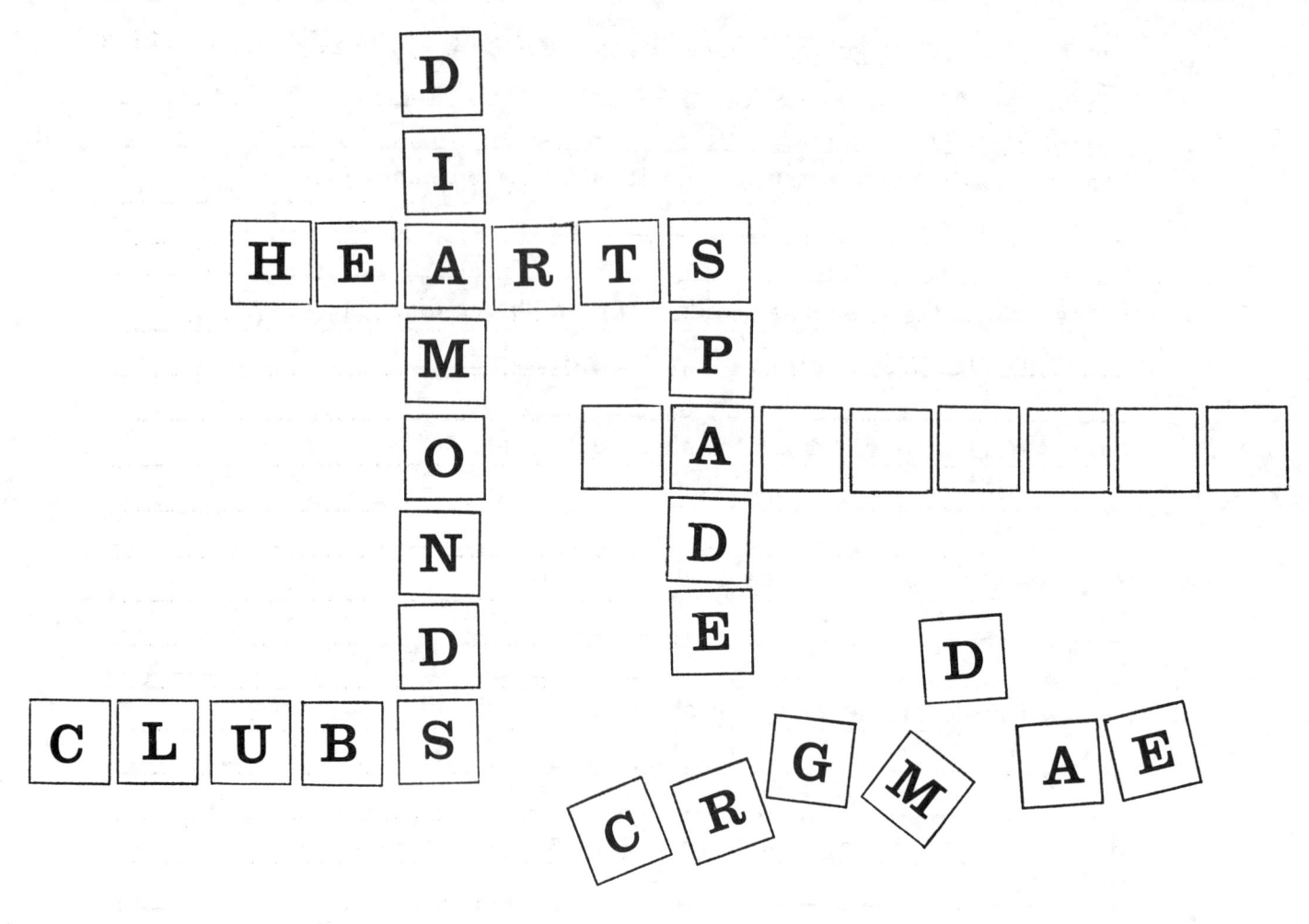

```
        D
        I
    H E A R T S
        M   P
        O   A □ □ □ □ □ □
        N   D
        D   E
C L U B S         D
              C R G M A E
```

Can you rearrange these Scrabble tiles so that the letters spell a word?

12. I won't play gin rummy with you because you won't watch what you're doing.
    _____
    _____

13. Because I didn't know you were such a good player, I never made you my partner before this.
    _____
    _____

14. Because the ante was so high already, I couldn't raise and see you.
    _____
    _____

15. I do well at Trivial Pursuit because I read so much.
    _____
    _____

16. I don't enjoy chess because it takes a lot of concentration.
    _____
    _____

51 Conditional clauses: unreal

B. Rewrite your answers to sentences 1–6 from Exercise A, changing the order of the **if** and main clauses.

I wouldn't bet on this bridge hand if I weren't a gambler.
If I weren't a gambler, I wouldn't bet on this bridge hand.

If I could have gotten one more heart, I could have won the trick.
I could have won the trick if I could have gotten one more heart.

1. _____
2. _____
3. _____
4. _____
5. _____
6. _____

Vocabulary Summary

ante	chess	hearts	set
backgammon	concentration	partner	solitaire
bet	dealer	pinochle	tile
black jack	do better/well	poker	trick
board game	fish	raise	Trivial Pursuit
bridge	gambler	score	trump
card game	gin rummy	Scrabble	
cheat	hand	see	

♥ Heart   ♣ Club
♦ Diamond   ♠ Spade

51 Conditional clauses: unreal   184

C. Complete these sentences about what you would have if.... Use the present time.

If I had one more king, I'd have four kings.

1. _____ a straight.

2. _____ a flush.

3. _____ a full house.

4. _____ a royal flush.

5. _____ a full house.

6. _____ a full house.

7. _____ a flush.

```
K K K K . . . Four Kings      A K Q J 10  ⎫
5 6 7 8 9 . . Straight        ♡ ♡ ♡ ♡ ♡   ⎬ . Royal Flush
♡ ♡ ♡ ♡ ♡ . . Flush           8 8 8 7 7 . . . Full House, eight high
```

Noun clauses 52

Possibilities

Hope talks about a possibility. **Wish** talks about a condition that doesn't or didn't exist.

> *Valerie **hopes** she can go to Bali someday. (She may be able to go.)*
> *She **wishes** she'd gone last year, when she had the chance. (She didn't go.)*

Contrast the verb forms in the noun clauses that follow **hope** and **wish**.

	hope	wish
present or future time	*I hope my plan **is** acceptable to you.* *I hope we **can** meet soon.* *I hope you **come**/you'**ll come** and visit us.*	*I wish my plan **were*** acceptable to you.* *I wish we **could** meet soon.* *I wish you'**d come** and visit us.*
past time	*I hope you **liked** your first taste of whale meat.* *I hope you'**ve enjoyed** the rest of the meal too.*	*I wish you'**d liked** your first taste of whale meat.* *I wish you'**d enjoyed** the rest of the meal too.* *I wish you **could have finished** it.*

*****Were** is the form of **be** used for all persons.

Hope can be followed by **so** or **not**, in place of a noun clause.

> *Is your mother-in-law going to be with you very long?*
> *I hope she is. / I hope so.*
>   or
> *I hope she isn't. / I hope not.*

52 Noun clauses with HOPE and WISH

A. Fill in each blank with a form of **hope** or **wish**.

We _hope_ you're having a good time on your vacation.

1. I'll bet Napoleon _____ he'd never seen Elba.
2. Maybe there's no point in _____ for what you can't have, but I still _____ I could live on a desert island someday. If I do, I _____ I find someone like Friday there, as Robinson Crusoe did.
3. I _____ so, too.
4. I _____ I could have seen your parents' faces when you told them your news.
5. What do you _____ to be doing ten years from now?
6. After I mailed the letter to Elise, I really _____ I hadn't. Now I'm _____ that she'll think it's a joke.
7. Where do you _____ you were right now? Where do you _____ I were right now?

8. Have you ever _____ you could have done things differently in your life?
9. Gary _____ he can retire soon. He _____ he didn't have to teach anymore. His students _____ he didn't, too.
10. I _____ you'd listen to me more often. I _____ you've been listening this time, because what I said was really important.
11. Milt _____ he and Zelda have another baby. Zelda _____ not.

187 Noun clauses with HOPE and WISH 52

B. Complete the sentences.

Bart and Maria went to hear La Traviata. Bart would like to hear it again. Maria is sorry she heard it this time.

Bart hopes *he can hear La Traviata again*.
Maria wishes *she hadn't heard it this time*.

1. Anabel and Claude are going out on their first date. Anabel thinks maybe they'll have a good time. Claude is sorry he agreed to the date.

    Anabel hopes _____.
    Claude wishes _____.

2. Claude and Anabel have had their date. Anabel doesn't want to see Claude ever again. Claude is sorry Anabel feels that way.

    Anabel hopes _____.
    Claude wishes _____.

3. Ted's Aunt Libby is coming to visit him and Felicia. Felicia wants Aunt Libby to stay as long as she can. Ted is sorry Aunt Libby is coming at all. Aunt Libby is sorry she isn't staying home.

    Felicia hopes _____.
    Ted wishes _____.
    Aunt Libby wishes _____.

4. Aunt Libby has gone back home, after three months. She's sorry she couldn't stay longer. She'd like to visit Felicia and Ted again next year, and perhaps she can. Felicia agrees. Ted doesn't.

    Aunt Libby wishes _____.
    She hopes _____.
    Felicia hopes _____.
    Ted hopes _____.

5. Aunt Libby is sorry she was so reluctant to visit Ted and Felicia in the first place. She's sorry she doesn't have more nephews like Ted. She wants Felicia and Ted to have a baby soon. It's possible that she remembered to tell them so. (She did, many times.) Ted is sorry Aunt Libby won't mind her own business.

    Aunt Libby wishes _____.
    She wishes _____.
    She hopes _____.
    She hopes _____.
    Ted wishes _____.

52 Noun clauses with HOPE and WISH 188

C. Use these illustrations to write sentences about your hopes and wishes.

hopes	wishes
_____	_____
_____	_____
_____	_____
_____	_____
_____	_____
_____	_____
_____	_____
_____	_____
_____	_____
_____	_____

Verb forms

Present	Past	Participle
become	became	become
begin	began	begun
blow	blew	blown
bring	brought	brought
build	built	built
catch	caught	caught
come	came	come
cost	cost	cost
do	did	done
drink	drank	drunk
drive	drove	driven
eat	ate	eaten
fall	fell	fallen
feed	fed	fed
feel	felt	felt
fight	fought	fought
find	found	found
fly	flew	flown
forget	forgot	forgotten
get	got	gotten
give	gave	given
go	went	gone
grow	grew	grown
have	had	had
hear	heard	heard
hit	hit	hit
hold	held	hold
hurt	hurt	hurt
keep	kept	kept
know	knew	known
lay	laid	laid
lead	led	led
leave	left	left
lend	lent	lent
light	lit	lit
lose	lost	lost
make	made	made
meet	met	met
owe	owed	owed
pay	paid	paid
put	put	put
quit	quit	quit
read	read	read
ride	rode	ridden
run	ran	run
say	said	said
see	saw	seen
sell	sold	sold
send	sent	sent
shake	shook	shaken
shut	shut	shut
sing	sang	sung
sit	sat	sat
sleep	slept	slept
speak	spoke	spoken
stand	stood	stood
steal	stole	stolen
sweep	swept	swept
swim	swam	swum
take	took	taken
teach	taught	taught
tell	told	told
think	thought	thought
throw	threw	thrown
wear	wore	worn
weep	wept	wept
win	won	won
write	wrote	written

Appendix   *Some nonseparable two-word verbs*

Verb	Meaning	Example
call on	ask to recite	*That teacher enjoys calling on sleeping students.*
come back	return	*She never comes back from school on time.*
come over	pay a casual visit	*Come over for lunch sometime.*
come to	regain consciousness	*She fainted from fright, but she soon came to.*
get along with	have a friendly relationship with	*That fellow seems to get along with everyone.*
get by	succeed with a minimum effort	*Do enough just to get by; that's his motto.*
get over	recover	*It took him weeks to get over the mumps.*
get through	finish	*I can never get through his exams in time.*
get up	arise	*He gets up early.*
go away	leave	*Please go away; I'm busy now.*
go over	review	*Let's go over the battle plans again.*
keep on	continue	*He keeps on talking until everyone leaves.*
look for	search for	*They looked everywhere for the lost child*
look into	investigate	*Detectives are looking into the mysterious death.*
look like	resemble	*She looks like her grandmother.*
look out	beware	*Look out! The roof's caving in.*
look up to	respect	*Young boys often look up to famous athletes.*
pass out	faint	*The heat was so intense that many people passed out.*
put up with	tolerate	*He can't put up with dishonesty.*
run into/across	meet accidentally	*Two old friends ran into each other on the street.*
run out of	exhaust a supply	*They ran out of gas in the middle of the Bay Bridge.*
run over	hit by a car	*The driver lost control and ran over an old man.*
show up	appear	*His ex-wife showed up at the marriage ceremony.*
take after	resemble	*He takes after his father in everything he does.*
take off	leave	*I can't stand this concert; let's take off.*
talk back to	answer rudely	*My children never talk back to me.*
wait on	serve	*He waits on tables for a living.*

A summary of verb tenses

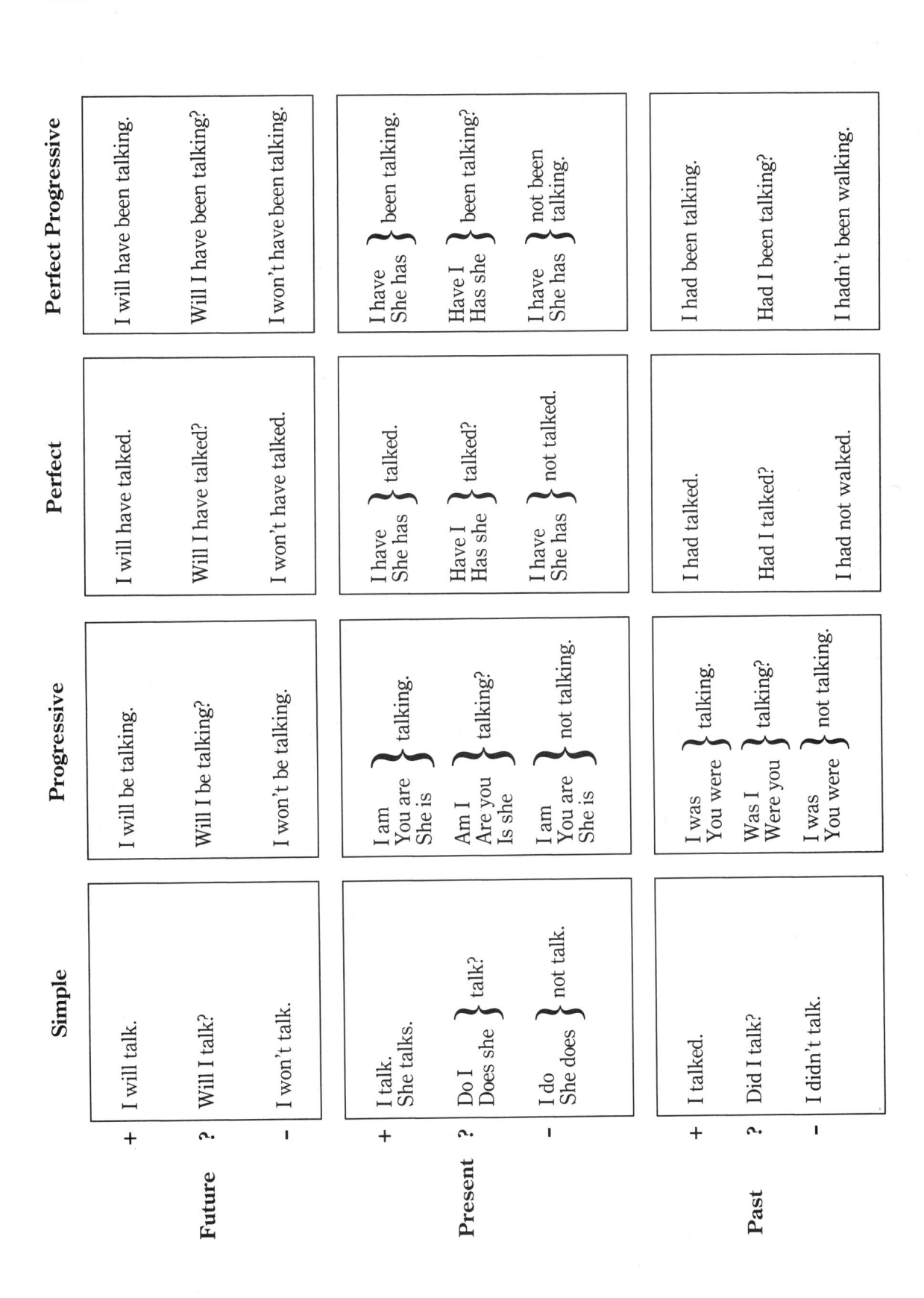

	Simple	Progressive	Perfect	Perfect Progressive
Future +	I will talk.	I will be talking.	I will have talked.	I will have been talking.
?	Will I talk?	Will I be talking?	Will I have talked?	Will I have been talking?
−	I won't talk.	I won't be talking.	I won't have talked.	I won't have been talking.
Present +	I talk. / She talks.	I am / You are / She is talking.	I have / She has talked.	I have / She has been talking.
?	Do I / Does she talk?	Am I / Are you / Is she talking?	Have I / Has she talked?	Have I / Has she been talking?
−	I do / She does not talk.	I am / You are / She is not talking.	I have / She has not talked.	I have / She has not been talking.
Past +	I talked.	I was / You were talking.	I had talked.	I had been talking.
?	Did I talk?	Was I / Were you talking?	Had I talked?	Had I been talking?
−	I didn't talk.	I was / You were not talking.	I had not walked.	I hadn't been walking.

Appendix *Some useful spelling rules*

A. If a word ends in **y** preceded by a consonant, change the **y** to an **i** before every suffix except **-ing**.

salary	salaries	copy	copying
marry	married	try	trying
lonely	loneliness	fly	flying
worry	worries	worry	worrying

B. Write **i** before **e,** except after **c,** or when rounded like **a,** as in neighbor and weigh.

    i before **e**: *brief, piece, chief, yield*
    e before **i**: *receive, deceive, ceiling, freight, sleigh*

Exceptions: *either, neither, seize, leisure, weird, species, financier*

C. If a word ends with a single consonant preceded by a single vowel (**hop, bat**) and you add a suffix beginning with a vowel (**-er, -ed, -ing**), double the final consonant when

    the word has only one syllable

stop	stopped	trip	tripped
bat	batter	drop	dropping
rub	rubbing	spin	spinning

    the word is accented on the last syllable

| occur | occurring | confer | conferred |
| admit | admitted | omit | omitting |

D. If a word ends with a silent **e** and you add a suffix,

    drop the **e** if the suffix begins with a vowel

| love | lovable | move | moving |
| desire | desirable | use | usable |

    keep the **e** if the suffix begins with a consonant

| use | useful | engage | engagement |
| love | lovely | move | movement |

Exceptions: words ending in **ee** never drop the final **ee**.

| agree | agreement | fleet | fleeing |

Answers

Lesson 1

Caption: A. piano B. trumpet C. cello D. harp

A.
1. Wasn't the Bach family the most important one in musical history?
2. Aren't Handel's oratorios the most inspired ones ever written?
3. Isn't the French horn the most beautiful instrument in the orchestra?
4. Wasn't Shostakovich's music banned by Stalin?
5. Doesn't the string section sound better than usual tonight?
6. Shouldn't the orchestra play more twentieth-century music?
7. Isn't Culture Club going to be in town next Friday?
8. Don't they have an excellent concert series here, for such a small city?

B.
1. Don't you like Billy Joel? I thought you did.
2. Isn't Jeff a Michael Jackson fan? I thought he was.
3. Didn't Brahms write more than four symphonies? I thought he had.
4. Won't you play a duet with me? I thought you would.
5. Wasn't Mozart older than thirty-five when he died? I thought he was.
6. Isn't the English horn a brass instrument? I thought it was.
7. Doesn't Barry Manilow like to be on TV? I thought he did.
8. Aren't you interested in music? I thought you were.

C.
1. Wasn't Ringo Starr the Beatles' drummer?
2. Don't you play a harp by plucking the strings?
3. Wasn't C. P. E. Bach J. S. Bach's son?
4. Didn't Segovia play the guitar?
5. Doesn't the piccolo have a higher range than the flute?

D.
1. Can't you play your drums a little softer?
2. Shouldn't that be played in the key of C?
3. Isn't it a good idea to get concert tickets in advance?
4. Shouldn't you practice the Chopin preludes?
5. Can't you play your violin tomorrow?

Lesson 2

A.
1. She told them not to miss the meeting.
2. She told them to be ready with the week's sales figures.
3. She told them to plan to stay no more than an hour.
4. She told them not to forget about the meeting.

B. Mrs. Graves says (that) she needs to make an appointment to have her hair done. She says she wants to look really special. She says she's going to an important dinner Saturday. Pierre says he can see her in an hour. She says she's sorry, but she can't be there then. They're having a big sale, and she can't leave the store. Pierre says he can give her an appointment Friday at 4:30. Mrs. Graves says that will be fine.

C. Mrs. Graves said (that) she needed to make an appointment to have her hair done. She said that she wanted to look really special. She said she was going to an important dinner Saturday. Pierre said he could see her in an hour. Mrs. Graves said she was sorry, but she couldn't be there then. She said they were having a big sale, and she couldn't leave the store. Pierre said he could give her an appointment Friday at 4:30. Mrs. Graves said that would be fine.

D. told, told, said, said, told, said, told, said

Lesson 3

A.
1. He's asking whether/if there are four quarters in a U.S. dollar.
2. He's asking why somebody gave him only three.
3. He's asking how many dollars he can get for a hundred francs.
4. He's asking whether/if anybody can change a hundred-franc bill for him.
5. He's asking whether/if the cashier will do it.
6. He's asking where he can exchange his French money.
7. He's asking what the name of the bank is.
8. He's asking how far away that is.
9. He's asking whether/if anyone wants to go to the bank with him.
10. He's asking what kind of friends he has.

B. Don said he was going Tuesday. Laurie asked (him) which countries he was visiting. He said Italy was the only one. He was staying with relatives there. She asked whether he had any Italian money yet. He said he was going to the bank for some on Friday. Laurie asked what kind of money they used there. Don said they used lire. She asked what the exchange rate was. He said there were 1920 lire to a dollar, according to the morning paper.

C. (sample answers)
1. . . . what kind of money they use in Austria?
2. . . . how many centavos there are in one cruzeiro.
3. . . . what the exchange rate of drachmas to dollars is?
4. . . . how many pounds you can get for one dollar.
5. . . . how many liras equals one dollar.
6. . . . how many kurus there are in a lira?
7. . . . what they use in Japan.

Lesson 4

Caption: A. lily B. rose C. orchid D. tulip

A.
1. How
2. What
3. How
4. What
5. What
6. How
7. What
8. How
9. How
10. What
11. How
12. How
13. What
14. How
15. What

B.
1. How many shrubs are you going to plant?
2. How's your vegetable garden doing this year?
3. What are doing that for?
4. How come you don't have any weeds in your garden?
5. What should I plant here next spring?
6. In what climate do apple trees grow best? (What climate do apple trees grow best in?)
7. How much time do you usually spend in your garden?

C.
1. How much are the flowers?
2. What kind of flowers are those?
3. How tall will this oak tree be?
4. How many shrubs are you putting in front of your house?
5. What kind of squash is it?
6. What color (of) dogwood is it?
7. How did you prepare your garden?

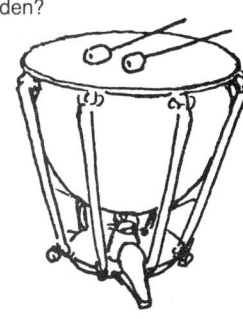

Answers

Lesson 5
(sample answers)

A.
1. Chang is from Korea, but Walther isn't.
2. Walther isn't from Korea, but Chang is.
3. Olga hasn't studied English for three years, but Ashraf has.
4. Ashraf has studied English for three years, but Olga hasn't.
5. Athanasios lives with his family, but Ricardo doesn't.
6. Ricardo doesn't live with his family, but Athanasios does.

B.
1.a. Consuelo can speak two languages, and Olga can, too.
   b. Consuelo can speak two languages, and so can Olga.
2.a. Hoa Thi lives with her family, and Chang does, too.
   b. Hoa Thi lives with her family, and so does Chang.
3.a. Ashraf has studied English for three years, and Julius has, too.
   b. Ashraf has studied English for three years, and so has Julius.

C.
1.a. Walther isn't from Mexico, and Hoa Thi isn't, either.
   b. Walther isn't from Mexico, and neither is Hoa Thi.
2.a. Consuelo doesn't live with her family, and Ricardo doesn't, either.
   b. Consuelo doesn't live with her family, and neither does Ricardo.
3.a. Walther hasn't studied English for three years, and Olga hasn't, either.
   b. Walther hasn't studied English for three years, and neither has Olga.
4.a. Chang doesn't speak three languages, and Hoa Thi doesn't, either.
   b. Chang doesn't speak three languages, and neither does Hoa Thi.

Lesson 6

Fritz: You were away for two months, weren't you?
Fritz: The trip was exciting, wasn't it?
Fritz: You're exhausted now, though, aren't you?
Fritz: You went to New York first, didn't you?
Manny: You haven't been there, have you?
Fritz: You didn't get mugged there, did you?
Manny: You think it's a dangerous place, don't you?
Fritz: That's surprising, isn't it?
Manny: People usually treat you the way you treat them, don't they?
Fritz: That's their longest-running musical, isn't it?
Fritz: You went to San Francisco from New York, didn't you?
Fritz: That's where they have those cable cars, isn't it? They weren't running while you were there, though, were they? They were being repaired then, weren't they?
Fritz: You don't expect to be able to stop, do you?
Fritz: You saw the Great Wall, didn't you? It was built over 2,000 years ago, wasn't it?
Fritz: You would have liked to stay longer, wouldn't you?
Fritz: That's where the Taj Mahal is, isn't it?
Fritz: That used to be called Constantinople, didn't it?
Fritz: There was a movie made about that, wasn't there?
Fritz: You can't take the Orient Express anymore, can you?
Fritz: You didn't spend all your time in Athens, did you?
Manny: I should have taken a cruise around the Greek islands, shouldn't' I?
Fritz: That was your trip, not mine, though, wasn't it?
Manny: You've been thinking about a cruise around the islands, haven't you?
Fritz: You didn't come directly from Athens to London, did you?
Fritz: Traveling is broadening, isn't it?

Lesson 7

A.
1. designer
2. director, producer
3. operator, programmer
4. painter, sculptor, dancer, singer
5. reporter, commentator
6. educator, administrator, counselor
7. editor, publisher

B.
1. electrician
2. beautician
3. technician
4. clinician
5. dietician
6. mathematician
7. statistician

C.
1. hygienist
2. a physicist
3. a journalist
4. a biologist
5. a chemist
6. a psychologist
7. therapist
8. a cardiologist
9. a hypnotist

D.
1. dentist
2. pharmacist
3. aviator
4. physician
5. optician
6. barber
7. janitor
8. teller
9. florist

Lesson 8

A.
1. yes
2. no
3. yes
4. yes
5. no
6. yes
7. no
8. yes
9. no
10. no
11. yes
12. no
13. yes
14. yes
15. no
16. yes
17. no
18. no
19. no
20. yes

B.
1. The, x, x, x
2. x, x, the
3. x, the, x
4. x, the, the, a, a
5. The, x, the, x
6. x, the, x, x, x
7. The, x, the, x
8. x
9. The, the, x
10. x, the, x
11. The, a
12. x, a
13. The, x
14. x, x, x
15. The, x, x
16. A, a, a, a
17. x, x, x
18. x, x
19. The, the
20. x, the, x
21. the, x, x
22. The, the, the, the
23. x, x, x
24. a, a
25. x, a, x, x

Lesson 9

1. yourself, yourself, themselves
2. himself, myself
3. himself, ourselves, oneself
4. yourself
5. itself
6. themselves
7. yourselves, herself
8. himself, himself
9. herself, ourselves, itself, ourselves
10. myself, yourselves
11. myself, himself
12. yourself

Answers

Lesson 10

A. 1. you, they, You, they, They, they
2. you, You, They, you, You

B. 1. We shouldn't honk our horns unnecessarily.
2. We should give pedestrians the right of way.
3. We shouldn't forget to signal when we're changing lanes.
4. We should always be careful to park between the marked lines in a parking lot. We shouldn't take up more than one space.

C. 1. One must come to a complete stop at a stop sign.
2. One must not park within ten feet of a fire hydrant.
3. One must not exceed the speed limit.
4. One must present one's car for inspection if it is ten or more years old.

D. 1. S
2. S, S
3. G, G
4. G
6. S, G
7. S, G
8. S, G, S

Lesson 11

(sample answers)
1. someone/somebody, anybody/somebody; no one; something, somebody, anyone; nobody; anything; everything; Everything; everything, something, anybody

2. nothing, Nobody, everything; something; someone; somebody/anyone, anything; anything; everything; no one; somebody

Lesson 12

A. 1. n't any; all
2. Neither; not, either
3. n't any; none, All
4. Both; neither, none, n't, any, both, all (See note.)

B. 1. were, were
2. Aren't, are
3. is, are
4. Is, was
5. are, know, play

C. 1. Another, The other
2. one, the other(s), another
3. the others
4. another, The others, ones
5. the others, one, the others

Lesson 13

(sample answers)

A. 1. Lots of the people said they enjoyed reading mystery and suspense the most.
2. A few/Not many of them said they enjoyed reading self-help books the most.
3. Not many/Some of them said they enjoyed reading literature the most.
5. Very few said they enjoy reading biography.
6. Quite a few said they enjoy adventure and romance.

B. 1. 5% said they don't get any enjoyment from reading.
2. 15% said they get a lot of enjoyment from reading.
3. 8% said they get very little enjoyment from reading.
4. 17% said they get quite a bit of enjoyment from reading.
5. 8% said they don't get much enjoyment from reading.
6. 19% said they don't get very much enjoyment from reading.

C. 1. quite a bit of
2. quite a bit of
3. quite a bit of
4. quite a few of
5. quite a bit of

D. 1. many, much
2. many, much
3. much, many

E. 1. Few, little
2. few, little
3. little, few

Lesson 14

A. 1. It's apparent, though, that you shouldn't expect to see everything in a few days.
2. It's a fact that there are almost infinite numbers of things to do in the city.
3. It would be advisable that you get around as much as possible on foot, because transportation is expensive.
4. It's a common perception that New Yorkers are always uncooperative.
5. It has often surprised visitors that they can be hospitable.
6. However, it seems to be true that the pace of life in New York is faster than it is almost anywhere else in the world.
7. It can fairly be said that a visit to New York will be an unforgettable adventure.

B. 1. On the other hand, it can be exciting to discover its wonders.
2. It may be more convenient to take packaged tours.
3. It isn't necessary to spend a great deal of money.
4. For example, it will save you money to buy half-price theater tickets at the kiosk at Broadway and 46th Street.
5. And it doesn't cost much to go to the top of the RCA Building, the Empire State Building, or the World Trade Center.
6. It isn't hard to find your way around the city.
7. It might be wise to avoid subways.

C. it take; It take, it took; it taken; it take; It takes, It, take

Answers

(sample answers)

D.
1. Mike: How long does it take to drive from Miami to Atlanta?
   Judy: It takes about 13 hours.
2. Mike: How long does it take to drive from Dallas to Los Angeles?
   Judy: It takes about 28 hours.
3. Mike: How long does it take to drive from Seattle to Miami?
   Judy: It takes about 66 hours.
4. Mike: How long does it take to drive from New York to Washington?
   Judy: It takes about 4½ hours.

Lesson 15

A. The following numbers should be marked with an X: 2, 3, 4, 6, 8, 9, 11, 12, 13, 15.

B.
1. a. Rehearsals for "Joe Egg" start this afternoon at 3:30.
   b. Rehearsals for "Joe Egg" are starting this afternoon at 3:30.
2. a. Marching band members leave at 10 for the state competition.
   b. Marching band members are leaving at 10 for the state competition.
3. a. Everybody going out for intramural basketball meets in the gym today at 4.
   b. Everybody going out for intramural basketball is meeting in the gym today at 4.
4. a. What time does the lecture end?
   b. What time is the lecture ending?
5. a. The archeology club has three guest lecturers next semester.
   b. The archeology club is having three guest lecturers next semester.

C.
1. The jazz group sounds so bad that I'm about to try out for it myself.
2. Have you ever noticed how many of our guest lecturers clear their throats when they're about to speak?
3. These school romances! Did you know that Harvey is about to break up with Tricia?
4. Poor Berta is so far behind that it looks as though she's about to have to drop out of the marathon.

Lesson 16

first paragraph: worked/was working, happened, was working/worked, started, called, got, was tearing around, was, were bringing in, were drinking, were, eating, were, noticed, was happening, began, moved/were moving, couldn't, went, suggested, got out of, was, were, talking, went, didn't, leave

second paragraph: was, was, was running, saw, were looking, were, laughing, was, didn't pay/wasn't paying, was going on, went on, called, whispered, did, dress

third paragraph: went, was waiting on/waited on, was giving out/gave out, said, was, didn't realize, wasn't talking, said, looked at, asked, Was, addressing, apologized, had to, was carrying, tripped, fell, landed, knocked, was sitting, dislodged, was, knew, was

Lesson 17

Caption: A. drill B. polishing brush C. polish D. water cup E. mirror F. probe G. hyperdermic needle

A.
1. s, specialized
2. haven't waited
3. has, been, ve taken
4. Have, had
5. ve used
6. ve, seen
7. Has, gotten
8. s, gone
9. ve, brushed

B.
1. How long have you had this problem?
   For almost a week.
2. You haven't hurt me yet, but I'll let you know.
3. Have you ever had root canal work done?
   No, I never have, and I don't want to.
4. I've just come from having a cavity filled, and the dentist gave me novocain.
5. Have you always taken such good care of your teeth?
   No. Since I paid $400 in dentist bills last year.
6. Haven't you started drilling yet, Doctor?
   These new drills are amazing. I've already stopped.
7. How many payments have you made on your bill up to now?
   All of them. I've finally made my last payment.
8. Have you lost this filling recently?
   Yes, it just dropped out yesterday afternoon.
9. How long has it been since the hygienist has seen you?
   I haven't had my teeth cleaned for about a year now.
10. How many times has your son been to the orthodontist so far?
    Let's see. He's been there three times up 'til now.
11. Has your dentist usually been on time for your appointments?
    I don't think he's ever started on time yet. He's run late every time so far.

C.
1. 've been
2. learned
3. has, had
4. has, told
5. have, seen
6. did, see
7. Has, bothered
8. was
9. did, hurt
10. Have, remembered
11. Has, experienced
12. did, tell
13. said, were

Lesson 18

A. Julius Caesar B. Charlemagne C. Mohammed D. Alexander the Great E. Cleopatra

A.
1. had become, killed
2. was, had taken
3. kept, had emerged
4. fell, had been
5. had already conquered, was
6. grew, had built
7. won, had already gotten
8. had made, declared
9. took over, had established
10. came, had appeared
11. began, had begun
12. had united, introduced
13. had controlled, cut
14. reawakened, had gone
15. had not yet seen, flourished

Lesson 19

A.
1. They will have met monthly.
2. They will have invited former faculty.
3. They will have tracked down all alumnae and alumni.
4. They will have sent out notices to everyone.
5. They will have hired a band.
6. They will have reserved the restaurant.
7. They will have worked out the menu.
8. They will have gotten a skit ready.
9. They will have made name tags.
10. They will have bought prizes.

Answers

B.
1. 'd been living
2. Have, been working; will have been working
3. hadn't been feeling; 've been feeling
4. Have, been getting along; 've been talking about
5. will have been working toward
6. 's been happening to; 'd been putting on
7. will have been wearing
8. 'd been trying
9. Have, been playing; hadn't been playing
10. Hasn't, been going out with; had been going out with, haven't been seeing
11. Have, been noticing, have been holding up; have been losing, have been losing

Lesson 20

A. Tim: used to do, use to play
Grandpa: used to be, used to play, used to spend, used to have, use to allow
Tim: use to watch
Grandpa: didn't use to be, used to listen

B. we'd often go, we'd carry, we'd swim and hike, we'd eat, we'd take, I'd fix, we'd put, we'd stop . . . and get, We'd go . . . and sit . . . and watch . . . and eat, we'd always have

C.
2. He's used to taking a shower in the morning.
3. He's not used to eating a good, balanced breakfast.
4. He's used to drinking more than two cups of coffee a day.
5. He's used to driving to work.
6. He's used to working all morning without a break.
7. He's used to carrying his lunch to work.
8. He isn't used to finishing work by 4:30.
9. He's used to getting home tired.
10. He's not used to going out in the evening.

D.
4. She didn't use to be afraid of flying, but now she is.
5. She's used to running at least two miles a day.
6. She used to sleep eight hours a night, but she doesn't anymore.
7. She didn't use to pay her bills on time, but now she does.
8. She used to swim regularly, but she doesn't anymore.
9. She's used to speaking in public.
10. She didn't use to study ancient history, but now she does.
11. She used to eat too much, but she doesn't anymore.
12. She's used to feeling ambitious most of the time.

Lesson 21

A. 1. b 2. a 3. b 4. a 5. b 6. b 7. a

B. 1. about to 2. going to 3. going to 4. going to 5. going to 6. about to 7. about to

C.
1. Benjamin and Colleen were going to move the accident victims when Wilhelm warned them not to.
2. LuAnn was going to study first aid, but she didn't think she had time.
3. At first Sybil and Sam weren't going to learn CPR, but now they're glad they changed their minds.
4. Delmar was afraid he wasn't going to survive when he realized he was drowning.
5. Foolishly, we were going to pick up a snake in the garden without knowing whether it was poisonous.
6. Daisy promised her mother that she was never going to take barbiturates again.
7. It was a relief to hear that the burn victims weren't going to die.
8. The inexperienced paramedic wasn't going to treat Cora for shock until he remembered that that should be his first priority.
9. When I felt heart attack symptoms, I was going to call my own doctor, but I called the volunteer ambulance squad instead because I thought they could get here faster.

Lesson 22

A.
1. You mustn't exert yourself in any way.
2. You must take these pills after each meal.
3. You mustn't have any visitors until Thursday.
4. You mustn't go back to your old habits when you go home.
5. You must take better care of yourself in the future.
6. You must quit smoking.
7. You must get more exercise.

B.
1.a. I have to see my father right away.
   b. I've got to see my father right away.
2.a. He has to have surgery in a few hours.
   b. He's got to have surgery in a few hours.
3.a. My brother and I have to talk with him before then.
   b. My brother and I have got to talk with him before then.
4.a. Do we have to get his doctor's permission?
   b. Have we got to get his doctor's permission?
5.a. We have to find out what the prognosis is.
   b. We've got to find out what the prognosis is.

C.
1. Yes, but I had to stay in the hospital for only three days afterward.
2. Did Mrs. Brewer have to go to the I.C.U.?
3. Yes, she had to have care around the clock.
4. Someone had to monitor her vital signs at all times.
5. Somebody had to call an ambulance.
6. We had to get Mr. Pangborn to the hospital.
7. He had to go to the E.R.

Answers

D. 1. Mustn't
    2. have to
    3. mustn't
    4. have to
    5. have to
    6. mustn't
    7. have to
    8. have to
    9. mustn't
    10. mustn't

E. Mrs. Duffy: Can I ask you some questions, Doctor?
    Dr. Wilcox: Yes, of course. You must ask me about anything that concerns you.
    Mrs. Duffy: Do I have to have an operation?
    Dr. Wilcox: Well, we might have to do a little exploratory surgery. Then we'll find out whether we have to operate. My feeling is that we don't have to do anything major. You mustn't worry, though; that would just make you feel worse.
    Mrs. Duffy: If I have to have the operation, what do I have to do?
    Dr. Wilcox: We usually put people with your problem on a mild tranquilizer. Then there are certain foods they mustn't eat, especially anything hot or spicy. They should also cut down on carbohydrates, although they don't have to avoid them entirely. And they mustn't smoke, or drink anything alcoholic or carbonated.
    Mrs. Duffy: Are you sure I'll be all right?
    Dr. Wilcox: Certainly. You must trust me.
    Mrs. Duffy: All right, Doctor. I'm in your hands.

Lesson 23

A. 1. They should dust the furniture.
    2. They should sweep, mop, and wax the kitchen and bathroom floors.
    3. They should vacuum the other floors.
    4. They should clean the bathroom.
    5. They should straighten up the basement.
    6. They ought to rake the leaves.
    7. They ought to mow the lawn.
    8. They ought to fix and paint the back steps.
    9. They ought to weed the vegetable garden.
    10. They ought to put up the storm windows.

B. 1. We'd still better clean the bathroom.
    2. We'd still better straighten up the basement.
    3. We'd still better fix and paint the back steps.
    4. We'd still better weed the vegetable garden.
    5. We'd still better put up the storm windows.

C. 1. You shouldn't walk on the kitchen floor while it's still wet.
    2. You should vacuum before you dust.
    3. You should throw away some of those old tools that you don't use anymore.
    4. You shouldn't use scouring powder on the tub.

D. 1. You'd better not walk on the kitchen floor while it's still wet.
    2. You'd better vacuum before you dust.
    3. You'd better throw away some of those old tools that you don't use anymore.
    4. You'd better not use scouring powder on the tub.

E. 1. Should I burn the leaves or put them out with the trash?
    2. Should I paint the steps gray or black?
    3. Should I use wax or oil on the dining room table?
    4. Should I put up the rest of the storm windows now or wait until Monday?

F. 1.a. You shouldn't burn the leaves.
      b. You hadn't better burn the leaves.
    2.a. You shouldn't paint the steps black.
      b. You hadn't better paint the steps black.
    3.a. You shouldn't use wax on the dining room table.
      b. You hadn't better use wax on the dining room table.
    4.a. You shouldn't wait until Monday.
      b. You hadn't better wait until Monday.

Lesson 24

A. 1. Would you rather walk or take a cab?
       I'd rather walk. I'd rather not take a cab.
    2. Would you rather visit the National Gallery tomorrow or the National Air and Space Museum?
       I'd rather visit the National Air and Space Museum tomorrow. I'd rather not visit the National Gallery.
    3. Would you rather climb the stairs to the top of the Washington Monument or take the elevator?
       I'd rather take the elevator. I'd rather not climb the stairs.
    4. Would you rather tour the White House or the Capitol Building?
       I'd rather tour the White House. I'd rather not tour the Capitol Building.
    5. Would you rather use a tour bus while we're here or find our own way around?
       I'd rather find our own way around. I'd rather not use a tour bus.
    6. Would you rather have lunch in a restaurant or have a picnic on the Mall?
       I'd rather have lunch in a restaurant. I'd rather not have a picnic on the Mall.
    7. Would you rather go to Georgetown or Arlington National Cemetery for a side trip?
       I'd rather go to Georgetown. I'd rather not go to Arlington National Cemetery.

B. 1. I'd like to visit the graves of John and Robert Kennedy.
    2. I'd like to look at the paintings at the National Portrait Gallery.
    3. I'd like to go to a concert at Kennedy Center.
    4. I'd like to see the embassies along Massachusetts Avenue.
    5. I'd like to watch a session of Congress.

C. 1. Would you like to visit the Supreme Court?
    2. Would you like to look at the models at the Patent Building?
    3. Would you like to hear one of the military bands play?
    4. Would you like to listen to people broadcasting on the Voice of America?
    5. Would you like to rest for a while after all this sightseeing?

Lesson 25

A. 1.a. Sure, and it can be prohibitively expensive, too.
      b. Sure, and it could be prohibitively expensive, too.
    2.a. A negligee can be acceptable.
      b. A negligee could be acceptable.
    3.a. I think it can be too personal.
      b. I think it could be too personal.
    4.a. That can't be the purse I bought you ten years ago. It looks new!
      b. That couldn't be the purse I bought you ten years ago. It looks new!
    5.a. Oh yes, it can.
      b. Oh yes, it could.
    6.a. It can't be our anniversary already!
      b. It couldn't be our anniversary already!

198

Answers

B.
1. a. This gold chain may be the perfect present for my nephew.
   b. This gold chain may not be the perfect present for my nephew.
   c. This gold chain might be the perfect present for my nephew.
   d. This gold chain might not be the perfect present for my nephew.
2. a. Mom may want flowers for Mother's Day again this year.
   b. Mom may not want flowers for Mother's Day again this year.
   c. Mom might want flowers for Mother's Day again this year.
   d. Mom might not want flowers for Mother's Day again this year.
3. a. Horacio may appreciate getting a gift certificate.
   b. Horacio may not appreciate getting a gift certificate.
   c. Horacio might appreciate getting a gift certificate.
   d. Horacio might not appreciate getting a gift certificate.
4. a. This shirt may fit Marcus.
   b. This shirt may not fit Marcus.
   c. This shirt might fit Marcus.
   d. This shirt might not fit Marcus.
5. a. I may be getting a car from my relatives for graduation.
   b. I may not be getting a car from my relatives for graduation.
   c. I might be getting a car from my relatives for graduation.
   d. I might not be getting a car from my relatives for graduation.

Lesson 26

Caption: The fish must be inside the cat!

A.
1. advisability
2. advisability
3. probability
4. advisability
5. probability
6. advisability
7. probability
8. advisability
9. probability
10. probability

B.
1. Inference
2. obligation
3. inference
4. obligation
5. inference
6. obligation
7. inference
8. obligation
9. inference
10. obligation

C.
1. It should be there now.
2. He should come back within a few minutes.
3. She should find them soon.
4. It should be snowing before long.
5. That should be enough for a movie.

D.
1. He must have a lot of free time.
2. They must enjoy music.
3. He must not believe my stories.
4. She must be studying late again.
5. They must not be speaking to each other now.

Lesson 27

A.
1. a. You're supposed to brush all tooth surfaces.
   b. You're to brush all tooth surfaces.
2. a. You're not supposed to rinse out your mouth after using Fluorex.
   b. You're not to rinse out your mouth after using Fluorex.
3. a. You aren't supposed to eat or drink for 30 minutes after use.
   b. You aren't to eat or drink for 30 minutes after use.
4. a. You're supposed to repeat this procedure daily.
   b. You're to repeat this procedure daily.
5. a. You're supposed to take 2 tablets every 4 hours.
   b. You're to take 2 tablets every 4 hours.
6. a. You aren't supposed to exceed 12 tablets in 24 hours.
   b. You aren't to exceed 12 tablets in 24 hours.
7. a. You're supposed to drink a full glass of water with each dose.
   b. You're to drink a full glass of water with each dose.
8. a. You're supposed to consult your physician if symptoms persist.
   b. You're to consult your physician if symptoms persist.
9. a. You're not supposed to take this product if you are allergic to aspirin or if you have asthma.
   b. You're not to take this product if you are allergic to aspirin or if you have asthma.

B.
1. Cressed toothpaste is supposed to prevent cavities.
2. Endopain painkillers are supposed to end discomfort fast.
3. Antisep mouthwash isn't supposed to taste unpleasant.
4. Buff headache pills aren't supposed to affect your stomach.
5. Nosneeze cold capsules are supposed to be effective for 12 hours.
6. Pouriton after shave is supposed to smell woodsy.
7. Ouchless burn ointment isn't supposed to get your clothes greasy.

C. 1. p 2. p 3. e 4. n.e. 5. o 6. n.e. 7. o

Answers

Lesson 28

Caption: I shouldn't have missed your Anniversity.
I ought not to have missed your Anniversity.

A.
1. I could have gone to college right after high school.
2. I could have bought the same coat on sale by waiting a week.
3. I could have said something really sarcastic in response.
4. I could have told him the truth about how he looked.

B.
1. You couldn't have paid $100 for that watch!
2. You couldn't have seen my name in the newspaper!
3. You couldn't have been eating without me!
4. You couldn't have lost the locket I gave you!

C.
1.a. I should have sent my landlady the rent check earlier.
  b. I ought to have sent my landlady the rent check earlier.
2.a. I should have let somebody help me wallpaper my kitchen.
  b. I ought to have let somebody help me wallpaper my kitchen.
3.a. I should have been trying to save money before I retired.
  b. I ought to have been trying to save money before I retired.
4.a. I should have spoken to the neighbors about their noise.
  b. I ought to have spoken to the neighbors about their noise.

D.
1.a. I shouldn't have quit my job without having another.
  b. I ought not to have quit my job without having another.
2.a. I shouldn't have forgotten my mother's birthday.
  b. I ought not to have forgotten my mother's birthday.
3.a. I shouldn't have been using your car without your permission.
  b. I ought not to have been using your car without your permission.
4.a. I shouldn't have slept for eighteen hours last night.
  b. I ought not to have slept for eighteen hours last night.

E.
1.a. I may or may not have misinterpreted what she said.
  b. I might or might not have misinterpreted what she said.
2.a. I may or may not have put the wrong letter in the envelope.
  b. I might or might not have put the wrong letter in the envelope.
3.a. I may or may not have swum too far out.
  b. I might or might not have swum too far out.
4.a. I may or may not have been eating the wrong things all my life.
  b. I might or might not have been eating the wrong things all my life.

F.
1. I must not have been concentrating on what you were saying.
2. I must have been standing in the wrong line for fifteen minutes.
3. I must have thrown away your gift by mistake.
4. I must not have heard the police siren behind me because I had the radio on so loud.

Lesson 29

A. 1. to 2. X 3. to 4. X 5. to 6. to 7. to 8. X 9. X 10. to 11. X 12. X 13. to 14. X 15. X 16. to

B. 1. we're not/we aren't able to 2. you may not 3. they didn't use to 4. I wouldn't 5. she isn't used to 6. they don't have to 7. you mustn't 8. we shouldn't 9. he ought not (to) 10. I'd better not/I hadn't better 11. they'd rather not 12. it couldn't 13. they may not 14. you might not 15. it must not 16. I'm not supposed to

C. 1. m 2. f 3. h 4. p 5. j 6. b 7. c 8. n 9. k 10. a 11. i 12. e 13. k 14. n 15. g 16. l 17. m 18. k 19. h 20. b 21. e 22. k 23. l 24. m

(possible answers)

D.
Anders: Let's speak English. It could be good practice for us.
Kiko: All right, I'll try.
Anders: Good. What are we supposed to do for English homework for tomorrow?
Kiko: That's right, you weren't in class today. How come?
Anders: I wasn't able to get a ride.
Kiko: Why didn't you call me?
Anders: I was about to, but I didn't want to bother you.
Kiko: You can call me any time. You should know that.
Anders: O.K., thanks. Next time I will. In fact, I may need a ride again Tuesday. Could you pick me up then?
Kiko: Sure, no problem. Anyway, the homework. We're to study the modal auxiliaries.
Anders: Oh no! Do we have to? I'd rather do almost anything else. I simply can't understand those modals.
Kiko: They ought to be easy. We've both been using them all through this conversation!

Lesson 30

1. brings them up
2. is looking for her
3. looks forward to it
4. keep off it
5. checked it out
6. picks them out
7. (are) looking into it
8. comes across it
9. takes it up
10. points him/her out
11. takes it over
12. has become of him
13. drop out of it
14. save it up
15. gets through with it
16. turns him down
17. hasn't caught up with it
18. runs over them
19. calls for them
20. hands it in
21. getting off it
22. to take them up
23. must do without it
24. pays it back

Lesson 31

A. 1. get 2. make, get 3. get 4. making 5. got 6. make 7. make, get

B.
1. Brite toothpaste will make your teeth whiter.
2. Sleepade will make you sleep like a baby.
3. Bloomalot will make your flowers grow twice as fast.
4. Teen Creme will make your wrinkles disappear.
5. Seethru detergent will make your dishes spotless.

C.
1. a. She had Bud adjust the brakes.
   b. She had the brakes adjusted.
2. a. She had him change the snow tires.
   b. She had the snow tires changed.
3. a. She had him fix the clutch.
   b. She had the clutch fixed.
4. a. She had him check the oil.
   b. She had the oil checked.
5. a. She had him wash and wax the car.
   b. She had the car washed and waxed.
6. a. She had him fill the gas tank.
   b. She had the gas tank filled.
7. a. She had him replace the battery.
   b. She had the battery replaced.
8. a. She had him change the air filter.
   b. She had the air filter changed.

D.
1. He's getting the carpets cleaned.
2. He's getting the walls painted.
3. He's getting the couch and chair reupholstered.
4. He's getting the stove replaced.
5. He's getting the windows washed.
6. He's getting new locks installed.
7. He's getting the curtains dyed.
8. He's getting air conditioning put in.
(These sentences could also begin "He's having . . .")

Lesson 32

A.
1. A hole can be burned in a steel plate by a laser beam.
2. "White" light is separated into a rainbow pattern, or spectrum, by a prism.
3. Radio waves are generated by electron tubes and transistors.
4. Radio telescopes are now being used by astronomers all over the world to study distant stars.
5. Light waves can be detected by our eyes, but radio and television waves cannot be seen by anyone.
6. Surface radio waves are weakened by contact with the earth.
7. Power is given to a gasoline engine by using air.
8. The mobility of vehicles on earth is restricted by gravity.
9. Statistics and how they might be manipulated by unscrupulous people should be studied by every consumer.

B.
1. The physical sciences can be divided into the two main divisions of chemistry and physics.
2. Now more than ever before, large amounts of inexpensive energy are needed.
3. Some cancer conditions are being treated with lasers.
4. In stereophonic sound, sounds are received from two or more separate areas.
5. More planets may yet be discovered.
6. A weak radio signal must be amplified.
7. The atmosphere above 25 miles is called the ionosphere.
8. Someday, communities will be built in space.
9. In space, a craft is being navigated in earth orbit.
10. It's easy to be misled about the meaning of a statistical "average."

C. Great break throughs will be made in science in the next few years. Much more is going to be understood about the history of the earth and the way it is changed by forces under its crust. A lot more will also be learned about the stars. The origins of the universe and of life will be understood by researchers around the world. The answers to these mysteries will not be accepted by all scientists, but those who don't believe in astrophysics and biological evolution will become less important. By whom will the wonderful scientific discoveries of the future be made? The Einsteins and Darwins of the next century may be studying in our grade schools today—in Brisbane or Hofuf, in Chongquing, Santiago, or Lagos. Nothing is known about them now; they are faceless nobodies. However, this can be predicted with certainty: The world will be changed by the next generation.

Lesson 33

A.
1. The lives of children with leukemia have been extended to as much as ten years by the use of drugs.
2. The woman's skin cancer had been detected by observation before it was confirmed by a biopsy.
3. Someone who has been stung by an insect can have a severe allergic reaction.
4. By the end of 1918, an estimated 20,000,000 people worldwide had been killed by an influenza epidemic.
5. In 1977, they found that "legionnaire's disease" was caused by a bacterium.
6. Adrenalin was discovered in 1901 by Takamine.
7. The first Nobel Prize in Medicine was won by von Behring.
8. The germ theory of disease was developed, the principle of immunity was established, and inoculation was originated by Pasteur.
9. Since ultrasound was discovered by Galton over 60 years ago, it has been used by medical science in various ways.

B.
1. Your throat cancer could have been cured before it spread.
2. The victim was supposed to be treated for shock.
3. The man was about to be pronounced drunk when he was identified as diabetic.
4. Bacteria were first described in 1676.
5. The Nobel Prize in Physiology or Medicine has been given since 1901.
6. The medical knowledge of the ancient Greeks had been preserved in Arabic, and then contributions from scientists of the Arabic Empire were added.
7. Since the discovery of DNA, the possibilities of genetic engineering have been studied and argued about.
8. Two ultrasonic techniques have been developed: A-scan and B-scan.
9. Ultrasound surpasses X-rays in searching for stones that have been formed in the body.

Answers

Lesson 34

A.
1. I'd work on building muscles, but I don't have any weights.
2. I know I should exercise more, but I don't care for doing anything very strenuous.
3. Why does everyone laugh at my planning to climb Mount Everest in three hours?
4. I like my doctor. She doesn't approve of anyone's working out with fancy equipment.
5. Exercising to build muscles is very different from exercising for health.
6. Thank you for holding my feet while I did my sit ups; I couldn't have done even one without you.
7. While all of you do calisthenics, I'll be in charge of counting.
8. I go to the gym because in addition to wanting to lose some weight, I'm interested in strengthening my muscles.
9. I refuse to exercise for fear of ending up in worse shape than I'm in now.

B.
1. Overdoing it is dangerous, though.
2. Beginning slowly and gradually building up the amount of effort you make is best.
3. Taking an exercise break during the day can be beneficial to your work.
4. Going through my exercise routine makes me tired, but doing so is worth the effort.
5. Working out with someone else is more helpful than doing it alone.
6. If going to the gym with your physique makes you embarrassed, accomplishing a lot right at home is possible.
7. Quitting jogging is tempting, but remembering the condition I was in before I started is correspondingly shocking.

C.
1. climbing a rope
2. doing sit ups
3. doing push ups
4. working out on the rings
5. doing chin ups
6. liftings weights
7. riding an exercycle
8. playing basketball

Lesson 35

1. He admits selling the brooch to pay off an illegal bet.
2. Mrs. Van Clee didn't appreciate losing her brooch.
3. Now she avoids going to dinner parties where she would have worn it.
4. Butch can't seem to help being a criminal.
5. He won't consider leading any other kind of life.
6. However, Butch denies ever hurting anyone while committing a robbery.
7. Butch enjoys breaking and entering for the excitement of being in someone else's house.
8. He'll finish serving his jail sentence in three years, with time off for good behavior.
9. He'll be glad to see the light of day again when he gets through doing time.
10. Butch's sister, Mae, used to be a thief, too. She's given up stealing since she got married.
11. Now she can't imagine breaking into someone's house.
12. However, Mae's husband, Dutch, keeps cracking safes.
13. Dutch will probably keep on being a safecracker until he loses his touch.
14. Mae doesn't mind having a safecracker for a husband.
15. When Dutch retires, Mae will miss getting nice surprise presents from him.
16. Dutch was going to go out on a job tonight, but he postponed going because he's coming down with a cold.
17. Instead, he'll stay home to practice finding safe combinations on his collection in the basement.
18. Mae and Butch have a younger brother named Algernon. He didn't have to quit living a life of crime, because they taught him differently.
19. Mae and Butch recall teaching Algernon to be the good one in the family.
20. They don't regret telling him that crime doesn't pay in the end.
21. Algernon used to resent being the baby in the family, and the only "different" one.
22. He used to beg to be taken along on a job, but Butch and Mae resisted taking him.
23. They didn't want to risk losing their baby brother.
24. Algernon wishes Butch would stop hanging out with burglars, thieves, and robbers.
25. In conversations with Butch, Algernon has often suggested his reforming.
26. Algernon can't understand Butch's associating with known criminals.
    Algernon forgets that Butch is in prison and doesn't have much choice.

Lesson 36

A. Column 1: planned, agreed, managed, seemed, refused, decided, hoped, tried

Column 2: hired, taught, advised, invited, encouraged, told, ordered, commanded

Column 3: expected, asked, would like, needed, prepared, begged, wanted, promised

B. Cross out the following: 2, 5, 6, 7, 10, 12, 14.

Answers

C.   I'll never understand teachers. Sometimes they seem to know everything, but other times they refuse to answer questions. They tell us to figure out the answers ourselves. They say that's because they want us to try to develop our own thinking processes, but I suspect it's because they aren't sure of the answers.

    Sometimes they're dictatorial. They command us to do this, they order us to do that, they forbid us to do something else. Other times, they're more considerate of our feelings. Then they ask or request us to do things, they encourage us to do our best, and they offer to help. They allow us to make mistakes, and that way they teach us to learn for ourselves.

    Even though I don't understand them, I expect to be a teacher someday. I hope to be the helpful kind, not the dictatorial kind. Students deserve to have the best!

Lesson 37

A.
1. a. I dread seeing my bills for photographic supplies.
   b. I dread to see my bills for photographic supplies.
2. a. When did you begin collecting butterflies?
   b. When did you begin to collect butterflies?
3. a. I've always liked fishing, but I've always hated cleaning the fish afterward.
   b. I've always liked to fish, but I've always hated to clean the fish afterward.
4. a. Do you prefer having sedentary hobbies or being more active?
   b. Do you prefer to have sedentary hobbies or to be more active?
5. a. I can't stand being interrupted when I'm looking at my collection of post cards.
   b. I can't stand to be interrupted when I'm looking at my collection of post cards.
6. a. I've decided that I'm going to start refinishing this old desk soon.
   b. I've descided that I'm going to start to refinish this old desk soon.
7. a. I used to enjoy hunting, but I couldn't continue doing it after I got arthritis in my legs.
   b. I used to enjoy hunting, but I couldn't continue to do it after I got arthritis in my legs.
8. a. Well, I never wanted to hunt or fish because I couldn't bear killing anything.
   b. Well, I never wanted to hunt or fish because I couldn't bear to kIll anythlng.
9. a. Some people love working on model airplanes.
   b. Some people love to work on model airplanes.

B.   1. c   2. a   3. g   4. b   5. e   6. f   7. d

C. Column 1: miss, enjoy, admit, regret, give up, suggest, quit, can't help, finish

    Column 2: ask, advise, decide, persuade, expect, tell, want, learn, hope, manage, force

    Column 3: start, dislike, continue, love, can't bear, hate, prefer, intend, can't stand, begin

Lesson 38

A.
1. They often get information just listening to people talk too freely.
2. Fred Shott, P.I., solved a case by hearing one person make an indiscreet phone call.
3. Her husband had noticed her acting suspiciously.
4. He hired Shott to help him get information.
5. The husband let Shott have a lot of information about her habits.
6. Shott saw the wife leave the house one day.
7. Shott was following her and observed her walking toward a phone booth.
8. At first Shott watched her talking to someone.
9. Then he crossed the street and overheard her making plans to meet someone.
10. She must have felt him listening to her, because she quickly hung up.
11. She pretended she was looking at some children playing across the stsreet.
12. But Shott had heard her planning a surprise birthday party for her husband.
13. Shott kept the secret and didn't let her husband find out about the party beforehand.

(possible answers)

B.   I watched the suspect enter a video game arcade. I followed him. I heard him ask the attendant for change. I heard him say he needed $5 worth of quarters. I saw him go over to one of the games. I watched him put quarters in the machine and begin playing. Soon I heard the machine making a cacophony of electronic beeps. I watched him play for a few minutes. I became entranced and forgot to keep alert for trouble. Suddenly I felt something hard poking me in the ribs. I heard a deep voice say not to move or else. I reached for my gun. I felt something crash down on my skull. When I came to, both men were gone.

C.
1. The little girl is watching the policeman walk along the sidewalk.
2. She doesn't notice the two men standing behind her.
3. The dog is looking at the little girl standing by the sign.
4. The policeman doesn't see the two men make the drop.
5. The woman is observing the two men exchanging something.
6. Fred Shott overhears the two men talking.
7. One of the men feels Fred watching him.

Answers

Lesson 39

A.
1. They have to do the dusting.
2. They have to make up the menus.
3. They have to do the shopping.
4. They have to make the guest bed.
5. They have to make plans for entertainment.
6. They have to do the best dishes.
7. They have to make some of the food ahead of time.
8. They have to do the laundry.
9. They have to do over the guest room.
10. They have to make up their minds whether to invite anyone else.

B.
1. make; doing
2. do; make, do, done
3. make; make
4. done; making; do, make
5. doing; making, done
6. do, do; making
7. made
8. make; make, do/make, does, make; did; did
9. do; doing
10. do; make; make; making

C.
1. make the bed
2. do the dishes
3. doing the cooking
4. make a cake
5. do the laundry
6. did the shopping
7. made a mistake
8. make an appointment

Lesson 40

A.
amazing, amazed
amusing, amused
boring, bored
convincing, convinced
depressing, depressed
disappointing, disappointed
disgusting, disgusted
exciting, excited
exhausting, exhausted
fascinating, fascinated
horrifying, horrified
interesting, interested
intriguing, intrigued
overwhelming, overwhelmed
satisfyng, satisfied
shocking, shocked
surprising, surprised
terrifying, terrified
thrilling, thrilled
tiring, tired

B. 1. amusing 2. shocked 3. tiring, fascinating 4. bored, interesting 5. disgusted 6. overwhelmed, convincing 7. surprised 8. exhausting 9. horrifying, terrified 10. intriguing, disappointed 11. amazed 12. excited, depressed 13. satisfying

Lesson 41

A.
1. different from, the same, like, different from, alike, the same as, he, similar to, similarly, like, like
2. alike, different, different from, differently, the same, the same as, as well as, like, similar to, different

(sample answers)

B.
Alfred is similar to Mr. Brown.
Sara is dressed the same as Sally.
Sara and Sally are dressed alike.
Alfred and Mr. Brown are similar.
Sara and Sally are dressed the same.
Sara is as tall as Sally.
Arthur is not like Alfred.
Arthur's and Alfred's sweaters are not the same.
Arthur is not so tall as Alfred.
Arthur is different from Alfred.
Arthur and Alfred are different.
Mrs. Brown and the twins wear their hair similarly.
Arthur and Mr. Brown wear their hair differently.

Answers

Lesson 42

A.
1. Pete: Are you still working?
   Henry: I don't work full-time anymore, but I'm still working part-time.
2. Mr. Eastman: How's your health?
   Mr. Lewis: Pretty good. I can't believe I'm already 75 years old. Of course I can't do a lot of things I used to do anymore. I don't drive much at night anymore, and I'm not the athlete I used to be anymore. But I still have all my own teeth, and my eyesight's still good. I still have all my faculties. No, I'm not ready to give up yet.
3. Manuel: Are you retired already? You still look so young!
   George: Well, thank you. I like to think that I haven't started to show my age yet.
   Manuel: You're lucky. Look at me: 45 years old and I already look ten years older. I've already got false teeth!
   George: You still look pretty youthful to me, young man, but then I've got thirty years on you. Everybody looks young to me!
4. Erik: You say your husband is 86? And he hasn't retired yet?
   Mrs. Potter: That's right. As far as I can see, he hasn't slowed down much at all yet.
   Erik: That's amazing. I'm 50, I'm already looking forward to retirement, and I've already slowed up a lot.
5. The Judge: How do you feel about getting older?
   The Teacher: Oh, there are things you can't do anymore, but there are still compensations. Have you ever read Tennyson's "Ulysses"?
   The Judge: I've heard of it, but I haven't read it yet.
   The Teacher: Well, in it Ulysses knows he's already coming to the end of his life, but he isn't ready to die yet. He hopes he can still go sailing with his men one more time. He says that old age still has "its honor and its toil." He's still "strong in will to strive, to seek, to find, and not to yield."
   The Judge: That's beautiful. I feel that way now, and I hope I still do when I reach the end of my life.

B. yet, still, still,
anymore, already,
still, yet, anymore,
still, already, already,
anymore

Lesson 43

A.
1. very, very, enough, too
2. too, enough
3. enough, too, enough
4. very, too, enough
5. enough, enough
6. very, very, enough
7. too, enough
8. too
9. too, too, very
10. Too, very

B.
1. small, enough
2. large enough, too large
3. too long, long enough
4. too, big/large enough
5. very, too tight
6. too, big enough

Lesson 44

A. 1. M 2. T 3. F 4. M 5. F 6. P 7. T 8. P 9. F 10. T

B.
1. You'll find the antique furniture on the third floor.
2. The new anthropology curator has worked hard to improve the collection.
3.a. Hilda doesn't like modern sculpture, so she happily ignores that exhibit.
   b. Hilda doesn't like modern sculpture, so she ignores that exhibit happily.
4. Turner's vivid paintings are always on display at London's Tate.
5. Peggy lives in Rochester, but for some reason she's never visited Eastman House.
6.a. Since the big robbery, someone regularly checks the museum's security system.
   b. Since the big robbery, someone checks the museum's security system regularly.
7. Shouldn't somebody dust off these fossils once a year or so?
8. I'd like to see the Etruscan art at the Villa Giulia someday.
9.a. The Huntington will soon be announcing a major acquisition.
   b. The Huntington will be announcing a major acquisition soon.

C.
1. When we went to Cairo last year, we saw the superb Tutankhamen collection at the Egyptian Museum.
2. The dinosaur skeleton was right here this morning. Where could it be?
3. People always seem to talk in hushed voices in museums.
4. A woman just ran out the front door with a priceless Ming vase!
5. Their collection of ancient Roman coins has been increased dramatically during the last year by anonymous gifts.
6. I swear I saw that Greek statue wink at me surreptitiously a second ago.
7. The painting that was always on that wall was recently defaced by vandals.
8. Mireille goes by the Louvre every morning on her way to work at the perfume factory.

D.
Lefty: Have you ever noticed the diamond they have on display at the museum?
Gill: Noticed! I sure have! I stop in at least once a week to gaze at it with awe.
Lefty: Well, have you ever thought about stealing it?
Gill: Get serious. I dreamed about it just last night. But there's always a security guard in front of it.
Lefty: There's never one at night. I know because I've been hiding after the museum closes for the last week. There's only one guard on duty all night for the whole museum. He walks past the diamond once every hour, but that's it!
Gill: So are you doing anything tonight?

Answers 206

Lesson 45
(sample answers)

A. 1. Manner: in small quantities
Means: by grinding, with millstones
Purpose: for cleaning your teeth
Association: pits of ripe tropical fruit
Measure: a spoonful of creme, by the handful
Capacity: as a curative, as a tooth paste
Accompaniment: with a glass of milk

B. 1. of, with, of, with, of, as, for
2. with, of, with
3. by, in, of, by
4. by, with, with, of, of
5. by, by
6. of, like, by, of
7. as, of, for
8. of, with, by, with, of
9. by, in, in, of
10. for, by, in, as, in, as, With, like, in

Lesson 46

1. on/upon, for
2. with, of, in
3. to, to, to, with, to
4. by/with, in, of, to, in, about
5. for, for, of, to, in, at/by, with, of, of, of, to, of
6. of, as, of, for, of, for, of
7. about/with, with, with, of, of, for, of, of, of; for/on, on, of

Lesson 47

1. Would you like to go to the prom with my sister, whose date got sick?
2. Isn't she the one that's/who's about six feet tall?
3. She's at least six inches taller than I am, which could make dancing difficult.
4. I think I'll go with Luisa, who's close to my height.
5. Personally, I like women that/who are taller than I am.
6. Chantal, whom I went out with for a year, is taller than my sister.
7. I have a friend that/whom/X I'd like you to meet.
8. He's a man that/who's not terribly good-looking, but that/who has a wonderful personality.
9. He's someone that/whom/X I'm sure you'll enjoy meeting.
10. He has a brother that's/who's a real hunk, but I'm going out with him.
11. What do you think about women that/who go out with younger men?
12. I think the same as you do about men that/who go out with younger women.
13. I have an uncle whose girlfriend is eighteen years younger than he is.
14. My cousin, whose boyfriend is nine years younger than she is, is really happy.
15. People should be able to go out with anyone that/-whom/X they like, regardless of age.

Lesson 48
(possible answers)

1. He was born on May 28, 1940, while his parents were living in Hartford, Connecticut.
2. His parents lived in Hartford until they moved to Windsor, Vermont.
3. When his sister was born, his parents were living in Windsor, Vermont.
4. While his parents were living in Windsor, Vermont, his siter was born, on August 4, 1942.
5. His parents have lived in Windsor, Vermont, since they moved there in 1941.
6. They moved to Windsor a year after he was born, and a year before his sister was born.
7. From September '43 until the war ended, his father was in the Navy.
8. His mother worked at the Upson factory while his father was in the Navy.
9. His mother kept working at Upson for a year after his father began working there.
10. While he was in high school, he worked part-time at a drug store.
11. After he graduated from Windsor High, he went to Colby College.
12. He met Jean while he was at Colby.
13. A year before he married Jean, he graduated from Colby.
14. He's been working at the shipyard ever since he and Jean got married.
15. Their daughter was born a little more than two years after he and Jean got married.
16. After he had worked at the shipyard for seven years, he was promoted to superintendent.
17. They lived in New London for nine years, until they moved to Waterford.

Lesson 49

A. 1. Niagara Falls is relatively small, although/though it's still very impressive, especially from the Canadian side.
2. Mount St. Helens hasn't erupted violently again, although/though it's been making ominous sounds and spewing some lava.
3. Because/Since the continent is extremely cold, no large land animals are native to Antarctica.
4. Although/Though earthquakes are awesomely able to destroy, fewer people are killed by earthquakes themselves than by the following tidal waves.
5. Many mountaineering groups use the 1850 figure of 29,002 feet for Mount Everest, although/though a figure of 29,028 feet was established in 1954 by the one has ever
reached the bottom of the Pacific Ocean's Mariana Trench, at 38,635 feet.
8. The world's largest island is Greenland (840,000 square miles), not Australia (2,939,975 square miles), because/since Australia's status is asa continent.
9. Although/Though the Sahara is the largest tropical and climatic desert in the world, the Rub al-Khali is the world's largest continuous sand area.

Answers

B.
1. Niagara Falls is still very impressive, especially from the Canadian side, in spite of/despite its relatively small size.
2. Mount St. Helens hasn't erupted violently again in spite of/despite its making ominous sounds and spewing some lava.
3. Because of the continent's extreme cold, no large land animals are native to Antarctica.
4. In spite of/Despite their awesome ability to destroy, fewer people are killed by earthquakes themselves than by the following tidal waves.
5. Many mountaineering groups use the 1850 figure of 29,002 feet for Mount Everest in spite of/despite a figure of 29,028 feet that was established in 1954 by the Indian government.
6. Many attempt to climb Mount Everest, but few reach its peak because of its altitude and dangers.
7. Because of its extreme depth, no one has ever reached the bottom of the Pacific Ocean's Mariana Trench, at 38,635 feet.
8. The world's largest island is Greenland (840,000 square miles), not Australia (2,939,975 square miles), because of Australia's status as a continent.
9. In spite of/Despite the Sahara's being the largest tropical and climatic desert in the world, the Rub al-Khali is the world's largest continuous sand area.

Lesson 50

A.
1. You should take a small gift, such as flowers or a bottle of wine, if you're invited to someone's house for dinner.
2. It's only polite to tell your hostess or host if you're not able to accept an invitation.
3. If you get something stuck in your throat at dinner, excuse yourself and leave the table.
4. It's impolite to ask who other guests will be or say, "I won't go if X is there."
5. If people have dinner together in a restaurant, it's not unusual for each to pay for his or her own meal, or "go Dutch."
6. However, if one person insists on paying for all, another can offer to pay the tip.
7. "Will you be offended if I'm not able to join you tonight?" is one rather formal way of declining an invitation.
8. O.K., I promise that if anyone brings up the subject of politics at dinner, I won't say anything.
9. Will you also keep quiet if they mention religion, another subject that shouldn't be discussed at the table?
10. What should I do if Selma and Jim serve us something I hate, like tripe or rhubarb?
11. If you're served a food you don't like, just leave it; don't make a point of talking about it.
12. How will you let me know if you think it's time to go home?
13. If you don't see me give you a meaningful look, I'll clear my throat and say, "Well . . . ," the way people always do when they're about to leave.
14. If I'm having a good time, maybe I won't want to leave. What will you do then?

B.
1. If you're invited to someone's house for dinner, you should take a small gift, such as flowers or a bottle of wine.
2. If you're not able to accept an invitation, it's only polite to tell your hostess or host.
3. Excuse yourself and leave the table if you get something stuck in your throat at dinner.
4. It's impolite to ask who other guests will be or say, "If X is there, I won't go ."
5. It's not unusual for each to pay for his or her own meal, or "go Dutch," if people have dinner together in a restaurant.
6. However, another can offer to pay the tip if one person insists on paying for all.
7. "If I'm not able to join you tonight, will you be offended?" is one rather formal way of declining an invitation.
8. O.K., I promise that I won't say anything if anyone brings up the subject of politics at dinner.
9. If they mention religion, another subject that shouldn't be discussed at the table, will you also keep quiet?
10. If Selma and Jim serve us something I hate, like tripe or rhubarb, what should I do?
11. Just leave it, if you're served a food you don't like; don't make a point of talking about it.
12. If you think it's time to go home, how will you let me know?
13. I'll clear my throat and say, "Well . . . ," the way people always do when they're about to leave, if you don't see me give you a meaningful look.
14. Maybe I won't want to leave, if I'm having a good time. What will you do then?

Answers

Lesson 51

Caption: CARDGAME

A.
1. If spades were trump, I'd have a good hand.
2. I would have done better if I'd had clubs or diamonds.
3. I'd be glad to play hearts if you were teaching me how.
4. You wouldn't have won the poker game if you hadn't cheated.
5. If some of the tiles weren't missing, we could play Scrabble.
6. If I had more friends, I wouldn't have to play solitaire.
7. We could play pinochle if we could find one more person.
8. You wouldn't have won at black jack if I'd been the dealer.
9. We could have played backgammon if I hadn't sold my set.
10. If it didn't seem so childish, I'd enjoy fish.
11. If you'd paid attention, we wouldn't have lost that trick.
12. I'd play gin rummy with you if I could be sure you'll watch what you're doing.
13. If I'd known you were such a good player, I would have made you my partner before this.
14. If the ante hadn't been so high already, I could have raised and seen you.
15. I wouldn't do well at Trivial Pursuit if I didn't read so much.
16. I'd enjoy chess if it didn't take a lot of concentration.

B.
1. I'd have a good hand if spades were trump.
2. If I'd had clubs or diamonds, I would have done better.
3. If you were teaching me how, I'd be glad to play hearts.
4. If you hadn't cheated, you wouldn't have won the poker game.
5. We could play Scrabble if some of the tiles weren't missing.
6. I wouldn't have to play solitaire if I had more friends.

C.
1. If I had a six, I'd have a straight.
2. If I had another heart, I'd have a flush.
3. If I had another king, I'd have a full house.
4. If I had a ten of hearts, I'd have a royal flush.
5. If I had another seven, I'd have a full house.
6. If I had another four or a two, I'd have a full house.
7. If I had another diamond, I'd have a flush.

Lesson 52

A.
1. wished
2. wishing, wish, hope
3. hope
4. wish
5. hope
6. wished, hoping
7. wish, wish
8. wished
9. hopes, wishes, wish
10. wish, hope
11. hopes, hopes

(possible answers)

B.
1. Anabel hopes they('ll) have a good time.
   Claude wishes he hadn't agreed to the date.
2. Anabel hopes she never sees Claude again.
   Claude wishes Anabel didn't feel that way.
3. Felicia hopes Aunt Libby will stay as long as she can.
   Ted wishes Aunt Libby weren't coming at all.
   Aunt Libby wishes she were staying home.
4. Aunt Libby wishes she could have stayed longer.
   She hopes she can visit Felicia and Ted again next year.
   Felicia hopes she will.
   Ted hopes she won't.
5. Aunt Libby wishes she hadn't been so reluctant to visit Ted and Felicia in the first place.
   She wishes she had more nephews like Ted.
   She hopes Felicia and Ted have a baby soon.
   She hopes she remembered to tell them so.
   Ted wishes Aunt Libby would mind her own business.

Grammar and key word index

about to 50, 72
abstract nouns 27
adjectives clauses 167
adverb clauses of reason and concession 173
adverb clauses of time 170
adverbials, word order 155
adverbs of degree 152
adverbs of time 148
advisability and obligation 79, 99
after 61, 170
agent suffixes 24
all 38
allow 131
already 57, 61, 148
although 173
always 155
another 38
anticipatory it 46
any 41
anymore 148
anyone/anybody/anything 35
as 53
as aoon as 61

because 173
before 61, 170
both 38
but 16
by the time 61

can 86, 95, 99, 185
causative 107
command 4
comparative constructions 145
compound pronouns 35
compound sentences 16
conclusion, modals of 95, 99
conditional clauses: real 176
conditional clauses: unreal 180
continuous 50, 54, 115
contraction 1
contrary-to-fact 180
could 86, 95, 180, 185
count/non-count 41
customary past/present 68

different (from) 145
despite 173
do vs make 139
do 68, 141

either 16, 38
enough 152
ever 57, 155
everyone/everybody/everything 35

few 41
finally 57
for 56
forget 131
future 50, 111
future perfect 64
future possible 176

gerunds 119, 123, 131
get 107
going to 50, 72

had better 79, 99
have 107, 135
have to 75, 99
help 135
hope 185
how 13, 56

if 9, 176, 180
imperative 6
impersonal pronouns 32
impossibility (surprise) 95
indefinite compound pronouns 35
infinitive 6, 46, 127, 131
inspite of 173
intensive 30
it 20, 46

just 57, 61

lately 57
let 135
like 145
little 41
lot(s) 41

Grammar and key word index

make vs do   139
make   197, 135, 139
many   13, 41
may   86, 95, 99
meanwhile   53
might   86, 95, 99, 180
modals   75, 79, 83, 86, 89, 92, 95, 99, 115
much   13
must   75, 89, 95, 99

negative   1, 6, 20, 35, 72, 75, 79, 86, 89, 92, 95, 123, 145, 148
neither   16, 38
never   57, 155
no one/nobody/nothing   35
none   38
noun clauses with hope and wish   185
nouns   24, 27, 46, 123

obligation/expectation   92, 99
obligation/neccessity   75, 99
one   38
other   38
ought   79, 89, 95, 99

participles   53, 56, 143,
partitives   38, 41
passive voice   111, 115
past participles   56, 61, 64, 111, 143
past perfect   61, 115
past progressive   115
past, modals in the   95, 99
perfect progressive   64
perfect tenses   56, 61, 64, 115
permit   131
possibility   86, 95, 99, 180
preference   83, 99
prepositions   160, 164
present participle   53, 143
present perfect   56
present progressive   50
probability/inference   89, 99
pronoun   20, 30, 32, 35, 46

quantity words   38, 41
questions, yes/no, negative   1

how and what   13
in reported speech   9
tag — review   20

recently   57, 156
reflexive   30
remember   131
reported speech   6, 9

same, (the/as)   145
seldom   155
-self/-selves   30
short additions   16
should   79, 89, 95, 99, 180
similar to   145
simple past   115
simple present   50
since   56, 170, 173
so   16
so far   56
some   41
someone/somebody/something   35
sometimes   57
soon   156
still   148
stop   131
subjunctive   180, 185
supposed to   92, 99

tag questions   20
tenses   50, 53, 56, 61, 64, 68
that   167
there   20
though   173
too   16, 152
two-word verbs, non-separable   104

unrealized ability   95
unrealized obligation   95
until   170
used to   68
usually   57, 155

verb + gerund   123
verb + gerund or infinitive   131
verb + infinitive   127

Grammar and key word index

verb + simple or progressive forms   135
very   152

what   13
whether   9
when   53, 61, 170
which   167
while   53, 170141
whose   167
who/whom   167
wish   185
word order of adverbials   155
would   68, 180
would like   83, 99
would rather   83, 99

yes/no negative questions
yet   123

Cultural topic index

Numbers refer to lessons, not to pages.

academic studies 7, 15, 32
accidents 21
advertising 27, 31, 45
appointments 2, 17, 26
art 44
automobiles 31

business 31

change 20
clothes 43
coins 3
crime 35, 38, 44
currency 3

dates 2, 26, 47
dentist 17
doctor 2, 21, 22
drawing conclusions 26
driving 10

education 15, 32, 36, 52
etiquette 50
exercise 34

family relations 20, 23, 25, 35, 38, 39, 41, 42, 48, 52
feelings 8, 9, 11, 29, 35, 36, 37, 41, 46
flowers 4, 25
food 4, 12, 16

games 51
getting acquainted 5
gift 25, 50
growing things 4

hairdresser 2, 31
headlines 104
health 22, 27, 33, 34, 42
history 18, 33, 42
history, ancient 18
hobbies 37
homework 29
hospital 21, 22
household chores 23, 31, 39, 45

imagination 20
injuries 21

jobs 7

laws 10
love 47

measurement 14, 43
medicine 27, 33
mistakes 28
money 3
museums 44
music 1
musicians 1

natural wonders 49
newspapers 104
New York City 14

occupations 7
old age 42

pastimes 20, 37, 46, 51
personality traits 8
picnic 12, 20
plants 4
plays 40
police 35, 38, 44
private eye 38

quotations 8

regrets 28
restaurant 16
reunion, class 19

sciences 32, 33
signs 10, 22
social relations 9, 11, 16, 19, 20, 36, 39, 46, 47, 50, 51
sports 20, 34
student life 13, 15, 29, 36
study habits 29

teachers 36
theater 40
tools 17, 23
tooth troubles 17
travel 6, 10, 14, 24, 49, 52

waiter's life, a 16
Washington, D.C. 24